Education in the Metaverse

How VR is Changing Learning and Training Explore how virtual reality is shaping the future of education

THOMPSON CARTER

All rights reserved

Table of Content

TABLE OF CONTENTS

4

INTRODUCTION

The Revolution of Learning – Virtual Reality in Education

The world of education is undergoing a radical transformation. For centuries, learning has been primarily confined to physical classrooms, where students and teachers engage in a largely static relationship with textbooks, whiteboards, and lectures. However, the emergence of **Virtual Reality (VR)** technology is changing the educational landscape, offering new, immersive, and interactive ways to engage students and enhance their learning experiences.

This book, *Education in the Metaverse: How VR is Changing Learning and Training*, delves into the profound impact that **Virtual Reality (VR)** is having on education today and explores how it will continue to shape the future of learning. As we journey through the chapters of this book, we will take a closer look at the mechanics, challenges, benefits, and real-world applications of VR in education. From the basics of VR technology to its role in K-12 classrooms, higher education institutions, corporate training, and specialized vocational programs, this book provides a comprehensive exploration of the possibilities VR holds for the world of education.

What is the Metaverse and Why Does It Matter?

Before we explore how VR is transforming learning, it's essential to understand the broader context in which this revolution is happening—the **Metaverse**. The Metaverse is a virtual universe where physical reality and digital worlds converge, offering an immersive experience that can change the way we interact with information, people, and environments. Education, as a traditional pillar of society, is already feeling the ripple effects of this shift.

The **Metaverse** represents a seamless integration of the physical and digital worlds, where users can access a fully immersive, interactive environment. In this space, students are not passive recipients of knowledge; they are active participants, collaborating with peers and instructors in real-time across vast virtual landscapes. This interactive and engaging model of learning is poised to revolutionize how we think about education—allowing students to learn by doing, exploring, and engaging in real-world simulations.

The Power of VR in Education

Virtual Reality, as a core component of the Metaverse, offers a truly immersive experience that textbooks and traditional classrooms cannot replicate. VR has the ability to bring abstract concepts to life, offer hands-on experiences in a safe environment, and provide a level of engagement that is simply not possible with traditional learning tools.

The magic of VR in education lies in its ability to provide **immersive learning environments** that are engaging, interactive, and often far more memorable than traditional methods. Imagine a medical student performing a **virtual surgery** or a history student walking through **ancient Rome**—VR allows them to experience learning in ways that text-based content never could. Students can **visualize complex concepts**, explore dynamic scenarios, and gain real-world skills in a way that is more immediate, effective, and compelling than conventional teaching methods.

In this book, we will explore the many dimensions of VR's influence on education, breaking down how VR is shaping both **traditional learning models** and the development of new **immersive learning environments**. From training

8

simulations in corporate settings to the evolution of remote learning in schools, the reach and impact of VR in education cannot be overstated. VR's ability to provide **hands-on, interactive experiences** gives it an unparalleled advantage in helping students truly understand and apply the material they are learning.

A Shift from Traditional Learning to Immersive Education

As we move further into the digital age, traditional education is evolving. The old model of passive learning—where students sit at desks and absorb information through lectures and textbooks—is being replaced by a new, **immersive approach**. **Immersive learning** involves using technology to engage students more deeply with the content, allowing them to become active participants in their education.

The shift to immersive learning through VR is already happening in classrooms, universities, and corporate training programs across the globe. Students can now participate in **virtual field trips**, **interactive simulations**, and **real-time assessments**, making learning more engaging, personalized, and effective. By incorporating VR into the curriculum, educators are finding that students are more motivated, more

9

focused, and more invested in their own learning experiences.

But the journey is far from complete. The road ahead is filled with potential, as VR continues to evolve and become an even more powerful tool in education. This book will explore what the future holds for VR in education, the barriers to adoption, and how schools and institutions can harness the power of VR to prepare students for the challenges of tomorrow.

Challenges and Opportunities in VR-Based Learning

While VR offers remarkable opportunities to enhance learning, it is not without its challenges. As VR becomes a more mainstream tool in education, there are several hurdles to overcome. The **cost** of VR hardware and software remains a significant barrier for many institutions, especially in underserved or developing regions. Additionally, educators may face challenges in integrating VR into their existing curricula, requiring new teaching strategies, specialized training, and the development of engaging VR content that aligns with learning objectives.

However, the **benefits** of VR in education far outweigh the challenges. The transformative potential of VR to enhance **engagement**, **motivation**, and **real-world application** makes it a valuable investment for the future of education. As technology continues to advance, we can expect the cost of VR systems to decrease, making it more accessible to schools and institutions worldwide. Additionally, as more educational content and teaching tools are developed for VR, the integration of VR into educational systems will become smoother and more seamless.

The Road Ahead: Shaping the Future of Education

The road ahead for VR in education is bright. As VR technology continues to advance, its potential to shape the future of learning grows exponentially. In the coming years, we will likely see VR become an integral part of the educational landscape, helping to redefine the classroom experience and make education more **interactive**, **personalized**, and **accessible** than ever before.

For future generations, VR will not just be a tool for learning; it will become a way of life—integrated into everyday learning experiences, creating immersive environments that bridge the gap between classroom education and real-world application. The next generation of students will have the opportunity to learn in ways that are more dynamic, engaging, and relevant to the world they will enter. Whether through virtual medical simulations, remote learning environments, or interactive field trips to historical sites, VR will open up new possibilities for students to **explore**, **discover**, and **engage** in education like never before.

A Comprehensive Exploration of VR's Role in Education

In the chapters that follow, we will dive deep into the role of **VR** in transforming education, examining its applications across a variety of contexts—from **K-12 schools** and **higher education** to **vocational training** and **corporate education**. Each chapter will explore the unique ways VR is reshaping traditional learning paradigms, the challenges educators face in integrating VR into their classrooms, and the opportunities that lie ahead as this technology continues to evolve.

By the end of this book, readers will have a comprehensive understanding of how VR is changing the face of education—offering both a roadmap for those looking to incorporate VR into their teaching practices and a vision of what the future of education could look like in the **Metaverse**.

Welcome to the revolution of learning—where the future of education is virtual, immersive, and limitless.

CHAPTER 1

INTRODUCTION TO THE METAVERSE AND VR IN EDUCATION

What is the Metaverse?

The **Metaverse** is a term that's becoming more and more prominent in discussions about technology, gaming, and now, education. But what exactly does it mean? At its core, the Metaverse refers to a collective, virtual shared space where users, through avatars, interact with a computer-generated environment and other users in real-time. Unlike the internet, which consists of different websites and platforms, the Metaverse is more like an immersive digital universe where the boundaries between the virtual world and the physical world are blurred.

It is a 3D, persistent world that's continually evolving, hosting both digital environments and real-world interactions. Imagine it as a virtual reality space, combining aspects of **augmented reality (AR)** and **virtual reality**

(VR), where people can meet, socialize, work, play, and learn, all while interacting in ways that are almost identical to the real world. The Metaverse is not just a single application but a universe of interconnected worlds.

Defining Virtual Reality (VR) and its Role in Education

Virtual Reality (VR) is an immersive technology that allows users to interact with a computer-generated 3D environment through specialized equipment, such as VR headsets, gloves, and motion controllers. Unlike traditional digital experiences on a screen, VR takes immersion to the next level, offering a more lifelike interaction, making the virtual experience feel real.

In **education**, VR is transforming the way students learn by allowing them to immerse themselves in simulated environments, providing hands-on learning experiences that would otherwise be impossible in a traditional classroom. Through VR, students can explore historical events, practice medical procedures, and simulate complex scientific experiments, all within a safe, controlled environment. By integrating VR, educators are able to offer practical applications of knowledge, rather than relying solely on theory and textbook learning.

15

The primary advantage of VR in education is that it creates an environment that engages students by immersing them in the material. Rather than sitting at a desk reading a book or watching a video, students can participate in their education in a much more interactive, memorable way.

Overview of the Shift from Traditional Learning to Immersive Learning

Traditionally, education has relied on passive methods of learning. These include lectures, textbooks, written exercises, and testing. While effective to an extent, these methods are often limited in terms of engagement and active participation. For instance, in a typical classroom setting, students might learn about the solar system by reading a chapter in their textbooks or watching a video. Though informative, these methods may not provide the same hands-on learning experience as VR.

With the advent of immersive technologies like VR, **immersive learning** has emerged as a revolutionary way to make education more engaging and effective. Immersive learning refers to teaching methods that use simulations, real-time interactions, and virtual environments to make abstract or complex concepts tangible. For example, in the traditional classroom, students might learn about the human circulatory system from a diagram or video. In a VR classroom, they could explore a 3D model of the heart and circulatory system from the inside, walking through blood vessels, observing the flow of blood, and even simulating real-life scenarios like heart surgeries.

This shift from traditional to immersive learning is being driven by advancements in VR technology, which makes such experiences possible. It gives students the opportunity to interact with content in ways that are engaging and impactful. Immersive learning has shown to improve student outcomes, as it caters to various learning styles and enhances long-term retention by actively engaging students in the learning process.

Real-World Example: VR Classrooms in Schools

One of the most exciting implementations of VR in education is the concept of **VR classrooms**. These virtual classrooms provide a space where students can attend class from anywhere in the world, all they need is a VR headset. These VR classrooms are being implemented in both primary and higher education settings, offering an immersive alternative to traditional remote learning methods.

For instance, **Ann Arbor Public Schools** in Michigan have partnered with **VictoryVR** to offer students virtual field trips. Students can visit places like the Great Wall of China, the International Space Station, or a coral reef, all from their classroom, giving them experiences that would be impossible to have through traditional teaching methods. The VR experience brings a level of immersion and presence that no video or textbook can offer.

Furthermore, universities are beginning to adopt VR technologies to create virtual campuses and classrooms. For example, **Georgia Tech** and **the University of Illinois** have been exploring how VR can make remote learning more interactive. In VR classrooms, students can interact with their instructors and peers in real-time, just as if they were in a traditional classroom, yet they can do so from the comfort of their own homes or from across the globe.

This shift to virtual classrooms helps break down barriers such as geographic location, physical disabilities, and even financial constraints, allowing students from different backgrounds to access the same high-quality educational experiences.

By looking at the Metaverse and VR in education, we can see that we are standing on the cusp of a new era in learning. From interactive lessons to immersive experiences, these technologies are shaping the way future generations will approach education, making it more inclusive, engaging, and impactful than ever before.

CHAPTER 2

THE HISTORY OF VIRTUAL REALITY IN EDUCATION

The Origins of VR Technology

The concept of **Virtual Reality (VR)** has evolved over many decades, with its roots tracing back to the early days of computer science and immersive simulations. While the term "virtual reality" wasn't coined until the 1980s, the idea of creating a simulated environment for users to interact with can be traced to the mid-20th century.

In the 1950s, early pioneers like **Morton Heilig** began experimenting with what he called the **Sensorama**, a machine that combined visuals, sound, and even smells to create a fully immersive experience. This was one of the first attempts to simulate reality using technology. Later, in the 1960s, **Ivan Sutherland** and his student Bob Sproull created **Sketchpad**, a revolutionary program that allowed for the first time interaction with a graphical display. This development paved the way for the creation of the first true

VR system, **The Sword of Damocles**. This system, created by Sutherland in 1968, was a head-mounted display (HMD) that projected 3D images, a key component in the evolution of VR.

Fast forward to the 1980s, when VR gained more recognition, thanks to **Jaron Lanier** and his company **VPL Research**. Lanier coined the term "virtual reality" and created the first commercial VR systems, including the **DataGlove** and **EyePhone**, which allowed users to interact with virtual environments through hand movements and visual displays. The technology was still expensive and complex, but it marked a turning point in the development of VR.

Early Educational Applications of VR

The educational potential of VR began to take shape in the 1990s as researchers and technologists began exploring its use in learning environments. Early experiments focused primarily on military, medical, and engineering applications, where VR could provide simulations of real-world scenarios that were otherwise too costly, dangerous, or difficult to replicate in the physical world.

In the realm of education, **VR began to be explored as a tool for enhancing learning by offering immersive, interactive experiences**. In the late 1990s and early 2000s, VR applications in education were primarily used in specialized fields such as medicine, architecture, and aviation, where training in real-world situations could be risky or expensive. For example, VR simulations were used to train **medical students in surgeries** and **pilots in flight simulations**, providing valuable hands-on experience without the need for real-life consequences.

At the same time, **virtual labs and simulations** were being developed for high schools and universities, allowing students to engage with scientific concepts and experiments in a virtual environment. Instead of conducting an experiment in a physical lab, students could use VR to manipulate molecules, observe chemical reactions, or explore distant planets—all without leaving the classroom.

Pioneers of VR in Education

Several key individuals and institutions were instrumental in shaping the trajectory of VR in education, laying the foundation for its current widespread use in learning environments.

- **Jaron Lanier**, often referred to as the father of VR, was a pioneer not just in developing the technology, but also in advocating for its potential to transform various industries, including education. His work at VPL Research brought the idea of VR to mainstream attention.

- **Tom Furness**, another VR pioneer, created the **Super Cockpit** system for the U.S. Air Force, one of the first to incorporate VR for training pilots. Later, he became involved in **VR research for medical education**, including **surgical training**, demonstrating the potential of VR as a tool for practical learning.

- **David J. Stork** and other early researchers in educational technology pushed the boundaries of how VR could enhance interaction with learning content. Their work demonstrated that VR could engage students in a way that traditional teaching methods couldn't, particularly for abstract concepts and complex, hands-on training.

- **Stanford University** also played a pivotal role in the early use of VR for educational purposes. In the 1990s, the **Virtual Reality Education Laboratory (VREL)** at Stanford developed educational VR

23

applications, such as virtual tours of historical sites and VR-based science labs. These projects allowed students to experience immersive environments that were not otherwise accessible.

Real-World Example: Early VR Experiments in University Settings

One of the most notable early real-world experiments in VR education occurred in the mid-1990s at **University College London (UCL)**. There, researchers tested a VR program called **"Virtual Reality Based Education"** to immerse students in simulated environments for learning purposes. The project allowed students to virtually visit historical sites, such as ancient Rome and medieval castles, and engage with them in an interactive manner. This marked a key moment when education moved from being a passive experience to an active, immersive one, utilizing the power of VR to bring history to life.

Another pioneering effort took place at **The University of Illinois** in the 2000s. The university developed a **virtual anatomy lab**, enabling medical students to study human anatomy by exploring 3D models of the human body, rotating and zooming in on organs and systems. This interactive VR experience significantly improved students' understanding of anatomy compared to traditional 2D illustrations in textbooks.

Additionally, **NASA's Virtual Reality Laboratory** has been an influential player in early VR experiments, particularly for training astronauts. By using VR simulations of space missions, NASA provided astronauts with the opportunity to experience realistic environments and situations they would face in space, such as operating spacecraft or responding to equipment malfunctions.

Over time, the cost of VR technology decreased, and its applications expanded into more widespread educational settings. Today, institutions of all kinds—from primary schools to universities—are increasingly adopting VR to provide more engaging and hands-on learning experiences. Early experiments in university settings laid the groundwork for the adoption of VR technology across various fields of education, contributing to the exciting transformations in learning we see today.

This chapter has laid the foundation by exploring the history and evolution of VR in education, showing how early applications and pioneering individuals have paved the way for the transformative role VR plays in modern learning environments. As we move forward in this book, we'll explore more contemporary applications and how VR is shaping the future of education in the Metaverse.

CHAPTER 3

HOW VR TECHNOLOGY WORKS

The Technology Behind VR: Hardware and Software

Virtual Reality (VR) is a combination of **hardware** and **software** that creates a simulated environment for users. These two components work in tandem to deliver an immersive experience, allowing users to feel as if they are interacting with a virtual world rather than just viewing it on a screen.

1. **Hardware:**
    - **Head-Mounted Displays (HMDs):** The most important piece of VR hardware is the **headset**, or **head-mounted display (HMD)**. The HMD is worn on the head and contains two small screens, one for each eye, that display the virtual world. These screens are often equipped with advanced lenses to create the illusion of depth and 3D images. The **resolution** and **refresh rate** of the

screens are important to creating a clear, smooth experience.

- ○ **Motion Tracking Sensors:** These sensors detect the user's head movements and adjust the virtual environment accordingly. This allows users to look around the virtual world, making the experience more realistic. Advanced tracking systems also track hand movements, body posture, and sometimes even eye movement.

- ○ **Controllers and Haptic Feedback: Controllers** allow users to interact with the virtual world. VR controllers typically have motion sensors, buttons, and triggers, and are often equipped with **haptic feedback**. Haptic feedback uses vibrations to simulate the sense of touch, creating a more immersive experience when interacting with virtual objects (such as feeling the vibration of a virtual door opening).

2. **Software:**

- ○ **Virtual Environments:** The VR software is responsible for generating the virtual world the user interacts with. These virtual environments can range from simple, static images to complex, fully interactive worlds. The software must be able to render detailed 3D graphics in real-time, responding to the user's movements and actions to maintain immersion.

- o **Game Engines:** Many VR experiences are created using game engines like **Unity** or **Unreal Engine**, which are powerful software platforms for developing immersive 3D environments. These engines provide the tools to simulate realistic physics, lighting, and sound in virtual spaces.

3. **Real-Time Rendering:** VR software must be able to render environments in real time, meaning that as a user moves their head or interacts with the virtual world, the software must adjust the images accordingly. This requires high processing power, which is why VR systems often require a dedicated computer or console to run smoothly.

VR Devices: Headsets, Controllers, and Accessories

To create an immersive VR experience, various devices are used, each serving a specific purpose in the system. The combination of these devices helps users feel as though they are physically present within the virtual environment.

1. **VR Headsets:** The headset is the most recognizable VR device. Some of the most popular VR headsets include:
   o **Oculus Quest 2:** A standalone VR headset that doesn't require a PC or console to run. It's known for its affordability and ease of use, making it ideal for both gaming and educational purposes.
   o **HTC Vive Pro:** A premium VR headset with high-resolution displays, precise motion tracking, and advanced sensors. It is often used for more professional applications, including education and training simulations.

2. **Controllers:** These devices are used to interact with the virtual world. VR controllers are typically designed to track hand movements and gestures, allowing users to manipulate objects or navigate the virtual environment.
   o **Oculus Touch Controllers:** These controllers are used with the Oculus Quest and Rift. They have motion tracking and haptic feedback, making them intuitive and

comfortable to use for educational purposes, such as virtual experiments or learning games.

o **HTC Vive Controllers:** These are used with HTC Vive headsets. The Vive controllers are equipped with motion sensors, touchpads, and triggers, allowing for precise interaction with the VR environment.

3. **Accessories:**

o **Haptic Gloves:** Some VR systems use haptic gloves to give users the ability to feel and manipulate objects within the virtual world. These gloves use vibrations and force feedback to simulate the sensation of touch.

o **Treadmills and Motion Platforms:** To simulate walking or running within a VR environment, motion platforms and omnidirectional treadmills are sometimes used. These devices allow users to move freely in a virtual space, further enhancing immersion.

o **Eye-Tracking Devices:** Eye-tracking technology can enhance VR by tracking where users are looking. This helps in rendering objects more clearly based on where the user's gaze is focused, improving realism and reducing the need for unnecessary graphical processing.

What Makes VR Immersive?

The true power of VR lies in its ability to immerse users in a completely artificial environment, making it feel as though they are truly "there." Several factors contribute to this immersive experience:

1. **Visual Immersion:** The most important factor in VR immersion is the visual experience. The two screens in a VR headset (one for each eye) display slightly different perspectives to simulate depth. By adjusting the focus and field of view, VR systems can make users feel as though they are looking at a 3D environment. The more detailed and realistic the visuals, the more convincing the experience becomes.

2. **Audio Immersion:** High-quality 3D audio enhances the sense of immersion by simulating how sounds behave in the real world. In a virtual space, users can hear sounds coming from different directions, such

32

as footsteps behind them or a voice to their left. This creates a more convincing virtual world and adds another layer to the experience.

3. **Interactivity:** Interactivity is key to making VR feel real. When users can move around in the environment, touch objects, or manipulate things with their hands, they become active participants in the virtual world. Controllers, motion sensors, and even full-body tracking systems allow users to interact naturally and intuitively, increasing the feeling of presence.

4. **Haptic Feedback:** The sense of touch is one of the most important senses for immersion. By using controllers with haptic feedback or even specialized devices like haptic suits and gloves, users can feel vibrations, force, or resistance, simulating the sensation of interacting with virtual objects. For example, if a user picks up a virtual object, they might feel a slight vibration or resistance in the controller to simulate the weight or texture of the object.

5. **Real-Time Adaptation:** As users move their heads or interact with their environment, VR software must adjust the view in real time. The faster and more

accurately this adaptation happens, the more immersive the experience will be. Delays or lag in adjusting the view can break the illusion and make the experience feel artificial.

Real-World Example: Oculus Rift and HTC Vive for Education

Two of the most popular VR systems used in education are the **Oculus Rift** and **HTC Vive**. These systems offer immersive experiences and are used in schools, universities, and even corporate training programs.

1. **Oculus Rift:** The Oculus Rift is one of the most accessible VR systems, offering a plug-and-play solution for immersive learning experiences. With its high-quality visuals and motion tracking, the Rift is commonly used in education for applications like virtual field trips, medical training, and interactive historical tours. **Oculus Education** has partnered with several organizations to bring VR learning tools into classrooms, providing students with experiences they couldn't have in the physical world. For instance, biology students can virtually "dissect" organs in 3D space, or history students can take a tour of ancient civilizations.

2. **HTC Vive:** The HTC Vive, known for its high-end specifications and precision tracking, is used in more professional and technical education environments. The Vive's room-scale tracking allows students to walk around in a virtual space, making it ideal for applications such as architectural design, surgery simulations, and engineering training. In one example, **architectural students** use the Vive to walk through virtual building designs, allowing them to get a sense of scale and space in ways that traditional blueprints or 3D models can't provide.

Both systems have shown how VR can be applied in various fields of education, from interactive history lessons to high-level professional training. By offering students the opportunity to interact with their subjects in a more tangible way, VR systems like the Oculus Rift and HTC Vive are revolutionizing education.

In this chapter, we've explored how the underlying hardware and software of VR systems work together to create a seamless and immersive learning experience. As we continue through this book, we'll see more real-world examples of how these technologies are transforming education across various levels and subjects.

CHAPTER 4

THE EVOLUTION OF LEARNING TECHNOLOGIES

From Chalkboards to Tablets: A Brief History of Learning Tools

The history of learning tools is marked by a gradual progression from traditional methods to increasingly sophisticated technologies. These tools have continually evolved to enhance the teaching and learning experience, improving both accessibility and engagement.

1. **Chalkboards:** For centuries, the chalkboard was the cornerstone of classroom instruction. Teachers would write notes, diagrams, and problems on the board, and students would copy them into their notebooks. This method was revolutionary in its time, offering a medium for teachers to communicate directly with large groups of students. Chalkboards allowed for dynamic, real-time interaction and enabled teachers to illustrate concepts visually.

However, their reach was still limited by the constraints of static images and text.

2. **Overhead Projectors:** As technology progressed, the **overhead projector** became the next advancement in the classroom. It allowed teachers to project written content or images onto a screen, providing a more dynamic way of presenting information. This tool paved the way for more interactive and visual learning, helping students grasp concepts more easily.

3. **Computers and Digital Learning:** The introduction of **personal computers** in classrooms in the 1980s marked a significant shift. Computers provided access to a wealth of information and resources that could be used for interactive learning. The rise of educational software allowed students to engage with content on a deeper level. **Learning management systems (LMS)** emerged, offering online courses and resources that students could access anytime, anywhere.

4. **Tablets and Smartphones:** Fast forward to the 2000s, and the rise of **tablets** and **smartphones** revolutionized education once again. Devices like the **iPad** and **Android tablets** provided a mobile,

38

user-friendly platform for learning. With thousands of educational apps available, students could interact with content in new and creative ways. Tablets also allowed for collaborative learning, where students could work together on shared projects or assignments using cloud-based platforms.

Throughout this evolution, the central aim of educational tools has been to make learning more efficient, engaging, and accessible. From the simple chalkboard to the complex digital tools of today, each advancement has contributed to making education more interactive and dynamic.

How VR Fits into the Bigger Picture of EdTech

Educational Technology (EdTech) encompasses a wide range of tools designed to improve the teaching and learning process, and **Virtual Reality (VR)** is now at the forefront of this movement. EdTech innovations, from simple software to immersive experiences, aim to enhance learning, making it more engaging and tailored to individual needs. Here's how VR fits into the bigger picture:

1. **Personalized Learning:** One of the main goals of EdTech is to offer personalized learning experiences.

39

VR enables this by allowing students to control the pace and direction of their learning. For instance, in a virtual chemistry lab, a student can experiment with different substances, observe outcomes, and learn from trial and error. VR provides a level of interaction that traditional tools can't, allowing learners to explore and engage with content in a way that suits their learning style.

2. **Interactive Simulations:** EdTech has long been about providing simulations—whether it's a math game or a virtual history tour. VR takes this a step further by offering highly immersive, realistic simulations. In a VR environment, students don't just watch or listen—they interact with the content. This interactive aspect makes learning more engaging and helps improve retention. For example, VR can simulate real-world experiences such as navigating a foreign country, conducting a medical procedure, or even flying an airplane—experiences that traditional educational tools can't offer.

3. **Distance Learning:** VR has also found its place in the rapidly growing field of **distance education**. With the advent of online courses and remote learning, students and teachers need new ways to

connect and collaborate. VR provides a solution by creating **virtual classrooms** where students can meet, interact with their peers, and collaborate on projects as if they were physically present. This helps reduce the isolation often felt in online learning environments and fosters a more engaging and collaborative atmosphere.

4. **Bridging the Gap:** While traditional learning tools are still valuable, VR represents the next step in the evolution of EdTech. Traditional tools like textbooks, whiteboards, and even interactive apps can be limiting in terms of engagement and real-world application. VR addresses this by providing an immersive experience where students not only learn but **experience** the content firsthand. For example, instead of reading about the solar system in a textbook, students can "visit" Mars, walk on the moon, or travel through space, all within the VR environment.

Real-World Example: VR's Impact Compared to Traditional Learning Tools

Let's look at a real-world comparison of **VR versus traditional learning tools** to understand how VR is reshaping education.

Traditional Tools in Science Education: In a traditional science classroom, students might study the human anatomy by reading a textbook and looking at diagrams. While these tools provide useful information, they are static and don't allow students to truly "experience" the human body. Students might struggle with understanding the spatial relationships between organs or how systems work together.

VR in Science Education: With VR, students can enter a **virtual anatomy lab** where they can manipulate 3D models of the human body. They can zoom in to examine organs, walk through blood vessels, and see how the cardiovascular system works in real time. This immersive experience leads to a deeper understanding of the content, as students can interact with the material and "learn by doing." For example, a **medical student** using VR could practice surgery in a risk-free environment before ever stepping into an operating room.

42

Traditional Tools in History Education: In a traditional history class, students typically read about historical events, watch documentaries, and participate in discussions. While these methods can be informative, they often lack the emotional engagement and personal connection that help students retain information.

VR in History Education: With VR, history comes alive in ways that textbooks and videos cannot replicate. Imagine students stepping into ancient Rome or walking through the streets of a World War II-era city. Virtual field trips allow students to "be there" and experience history firsthand, fostering a deeper emotional connection to the material. Students can interact with virtual historical figures, visit landmarks, and understand events from a first-person perspective.

Traditional Tools in Geography Education: In geography classes, students might learn about different countries, landmarks, and cultures through maps, videos, and textbooks. While these tools provide useful information, they lack the ability to fully immerse students in the environments they are studying.

VR in Geography Education: In VR, students can travel the world without ever leaving their classroom. They can visit the Great Wall of China, explore the Amazon Rainforest, or hike through the Swiss Alps—all within a virtual environment. This kind of immersive learning offers a deeper understanding of geography by allowing students to experience the environments they are studying, rather than just reading about them.

This chapter highlights how learning technologies have evolved from basic tools like chalkboards to advanced systems like VR, which offer immersive and interactive experiences. While traditional tools still play an important role in education, VR represents a transformative leap forward, bringing subjects to life and offering students more dynamic, engaging, and effective ways to learn. As we continue exploring the potential of VR in education, the comparison to traditional methods will become even clearer in its ability to enhance student engagement and learning outcomes.

CHAPTER 5

KEY BENEFITS OF VR IN EDUCATION

Engaging and Immersive Learning Experiences

One of the most compelling reasons for integrating **Virtual Reality (VR)** into education is its ability to create **engaging and immersive learning experiences**. Traditional classroom settings often struggle to maintain the attention of students, especially when dealing with complex or abstract subjects. VR breaks down these barriers by pulling students into environments where learning is interactive and dynamic.

Immersion is the key to this experience. In VR, students are not passive recipients of information. Instead, they are active participants in a simulated environment where they can explore, interact, and learn firsthand. This level of engagement is unmatched by traditional methods such as reading from textbooks or watching videos. With VR, students feel as if they are truly present in the content they are studying.

For example, instead of merely reading about ancient Egypt in a history class, students can step into a VR simulation where they walk through the pyramids, interact with ancient artifacts, and experience the culture of the time. This immersion not only makes learning more fun but also more memorable, as it taps into the brain's natural ability to retain experiences involving strong sensory input.

Real-World Example:

- **The "Google Expeditions" app** offers immersive VR field trips that allow students to visit places like the **Great Wall of China** or the **Amazon Rainforest** from the classroom. By using VR headsets, students are no longer limited by geography—they can explore the world in ways that weren't previously possible.

Enhancing Retention and Comprehension

One of the key benefits of VR in education is its ability to significantly improve **retention and comprehension** of complex material. Research shows that when students are immersed in a learning environment, they are more likely to remember information and understand it deeply. This is largely because VR leverages multiple sensory inputs—visual, auditory, and sometimes even haptic feedback—which help reinforce learning.

Active Learning: VR encourages **active learning**, which is far more effective than passive methods such as listening to lectures or reading. In a VR environment, students can interact with the content by touching, moving, and manipulating objects or elements. These hands-on experiences not only help with comprehension but also make it easier for students to retain the information long-term.

- For instance, in a VR biology lesson, students can manipulate molecules and watch how they interact. By seeing the structure and behavior of molecules firsthand, students are likely to remember the concepts better than if they had simply read about them in a textbook.

Moreover, VR can cater to different learning styles. Visual learners benefit from the vivid 3D environments, kinesthetic learners gain from physical interaction with virtual objects,

47

and auditory learners benefit from the sounds and explanations provided within VR simulations.

Real-World Example:

- **Labster** is a company that creates **VR-based science labs**. With Labster, students can engage in virtual chemistry, biology, and physics experiments, exploring complex concepts such as cellular processes or chemical reactions in an immersive, hands-on environment. These experiences enhance both understanding and retention by enabling students to conduct experiments in ways that would be difficult or unsafe in a physical lab.

Encouraging Active Participation

One of the greatest strengths of VR in education is its ability to encourage **active participation**. Traditional education often involves students sitting passively while the teacher imparts information. In contrast, VR transforms students from passive observers to active participants in their own learning journey.

In a VR environment, students take the lead—they move, make decisions, and solve problems within the virtual world.

This active engagement helps reinforce learning and encourages students to take ownership of their education. By performing tasks or solving problems, students not only learn the material but also develop critical thinking and problem-solving skills.

For example, in a virtual classroom, students could work together on a group project, where they build structures, conduct research, or even solve complex puzzles, much like they would in a real-world scenario. This level of involvement helps develop key skills like teamwork, leadership, and collaboration, which are often difficult to foster in a traditional classroom setting.

Real-World Example:

- **ClassVR**, a classroom VR solution, provides a range of interactive VR experiences where students engage in active learning. Students can solve math problems in a virtual world, explore the human body by navigating through 3D organs, or conduct virtual archaeological digs. These activities not only engage students but also prompt them to think critically and collaborate with peers in a shared virtual environment.

49

Real-World Example: VR-Enabled Labs and Simulations in Science

One of the most significant contributions of VR in education has been in **STEM (Science, Technology, Engineering, and Math)** fields, where VR is making complex concepts more accessible and interactive. **VR-enabled labs** and **simulations** in science allow students to conduct experiments, explore scientific concepts, and interact with models of processes that would be impossible or too costly in the real world.

1. **Virtual Science Labs:** VR allows students to conduct experiments without the need for expensive equipment or potentially dangerous chemicals. For instance, students can mix chemicals in a virtual lab to observe reactions, experiment with various scientific instruments, or even explore outer space. These virtual labs are invaluable in educational settings where access to physical labs is limited or when it's too costly to provide students with access to certain materials.

2. **Simulating High-Risk Environments:** VR also enables simulations of environments that are either dangerous or impractical to replicate in real life. For

example, students can simulate dangerous procedures in a virtual hospital or practice solving engineering problems in a VR version of a nuclear power plant. This allows for **safe, risk-free learning** while ensuring students develop the necessary skills to succeed in high-risk fields.

3. **Building Complex Models:** In subjects like **astronomy** or **molecular biology**, VR can allow students to build and manipulate complex models. For example, students can construct virtual DNA strands, view them from different angles, and manipulate them to observe how genetic changes impact the organism. This hands-on experience enhances understanding and allows students to grasp complex topics in a tangible way.

Real-World Example:

- **Labster** offers a variety of **VR-based science labs** where students can conduct interactive experiments in a range of subjects including **genetics**, **biochemistry**, and **physics**. These virtual simulations are not only engaging but also ensure that students have access to high-quality labs and experiments that they might not have access to in a traditional classroom due to resource limitations. By engaging in these VR labs, students gain practical knowledge that is essential for future scientific and medical careers.

This chapter has explored the **key benefits of VR in education**, from creating immersive and engaging experiences to improving retention, comprehension, and encouraging active participation. By integrating VR into educational settings, teachers can provide hands-on learning opportunities that make complex topics more accessible and engaging. The real-world examples of VR labs and simulations in science show just how transformative these technologies can be in reshaping the future of education. As we move forward, the impact of VR in education will continue to grow, offering limitless possibilities for both students and educators alike.

CHAPTER 6

THE RISE OF THE METAVERSE

What is the Metaverse?

The **Metaverse** is often referred to as the next evolution of the internet—an interconnected, immersive virtual space where people can interact with each other and digital environments in real-time. It's a digital universe that merges the physical world with virtual reality (VR), augmented reality (AR), and other digital experiences to create an all-encompassing virtual environment.

In the simplest terms, the Metaverse is a shared, persistent virtual space where individuals can socialize, work, play, and even learn. Unlike traditional websites or apps, the Metaverse operates as a fully immersive, interactive environment that users can access through VR headsets, computers, and even mobile devices.

The core concept of the Metaverse isn't just about virtual worlds—it's about interconnected, **persistent virtual spaces** that users can explore, build, and interact with over time. These worlds are not isolated but interconnected, creating a digital ecosystem where activities can span across various virtual realms. The Metaverse aims to provide users with a sense of presence and immersion, allowing them to interact with others and digital content in much the same way they would in the real world.

Virtual Worlds, Social VR, and Their Role in Learning

Virtual worlds are at the heart of the Metaverse. These are computer-generated environments where users can interact with each other and objects in real-time. Virtual worlds can be anything from fantasy settings to realistic representations of real-world locations. They form the foundation for a rich and interactive learning experience in the Metaverse.

1. **Virtual Worlds as Learning Spaces:** Virtual worlds allow educators to create custom learning environments where students can engage with the content in unique ways. Instead of learning from textbooks or videos, students can physically interact with their subjects in 3D environments. For instance, students can explore a **virtual ancient Rome**, examine **3D models of the human brain**, or participate in **virtual physics experiments**. These

54

worlds can also support multi-user experiences, where groups of students collaborate on projects, solve problems together, or complete tasks in virtual settings that mimic real-life scenarios.

2. **Social VR for Learning: Social VR** extends virtual worlds into spaces where users can connect with each other in real time. This adds a social dimension to learning in the Metaverse. Students can attend virtual classrooms, participate in discussions, and interact with peers and instructors in a more personal and engaging way. The collaborative nature of social VR helps enhance **social learning**—a process where individuals learn through interaction, communication, and collaboration with others.

3. **Breaking Geographical Barriers:** One of the most powerful aspects of virtual worlds and social VR is their ability to break down geographical barriers. Students from different parts of the world can come together in a shared virtual environment, eliminating the constraints of physical location. This means that anyone with access to VR technology can participate in global learning experiences, attend virtual lectures, or visit educational institutions, regardless of where they are physically located.

4. **Cultural and Language Exploration:** Social VR also opens the door for cultural and language exchange. Virtual worlds can host **multi-lingual environments** where students can practice language skills or learn about different cultures by interacting with people from all over the world. These virtual interactions promote cross-cultural understanding, global awareness, and can help enhance language proficiency by immersing learners in conversational settings.

How VR is Expanding into the Metaverse

Virtual Reality (VR) is one of the primary technologies enabling the rise of the Metaverse. It provides the immersion, interaction, and sensory feedback needed to make virtual environments feel "real." Here's how VR is expanding into the Metaverse:

1. **Creating Persistent Virtual Environments:** VR allows for the creation of **persistent, interactive virtual worlds** that exist continuously, even when users log off. These environments can be anything from virtual classrooms and cities to training simulations and interactive museums. VR's

immersive capabilities enable users to interact with these environments in ways that go beyond just observing—students can touch, move, manipulate, and experience virtual objects.

2. **Bringing Real-Life Experiences into the Metaverse:**

Through VR, real-world experiences are being transported into the Metaverse. This includes things like virtual field trips to historic landmarks, interactive science labs, or architectural tours of famous buildings. VR technology allows users to experience these settings as though they were physically there, providing valuable learning opportunities that would be hard to replicate in a traditional classroom.

3. **Integrating 3D Interaction with Learning Content:**

Traditional education methods often rely on 2D materials, such as books, screens, or documents. VR introduces **3D interaction** with learning content. Students can "enter" the virtual environment and interact with the material. For example, in a history lesson, they can walk through a virtual medieval village, or in a biology class, they can examine the human body from every angle. This level of interactivity increases engagement and makes complex topics easier to understand.

4. **VR as a Gateway to Multi-User Interactions in the Metaverse:**

   VR makes it possible for multiple users to exist and interact in the same virtual environment, allowing for shared learning experiences. For example, students in a VR classroom can attend a lecture while sitting together in a virtual space, interact with each other through avatars, and engage in real-time discussions. VR's multi-user capability enhances collaborative learning, where students from diverse backgrounds can work together on projects and assignments in a seamless virtual environment.

5. **Virtual Avatars and Identity:**

   In the Metaverse, users are represented by **avatars**, which are digital representations of themselves. In educational settings, avatars allow students to interact in virtual spaces as they would in the real world. VR technology enables highly detailed avatars, which can include personalized features such as facial expressions, gestures, and body language. This adds a sense of presence and engagement, as users can physically move around virtual spaces, interact with others, and convey emotions and thoughts non-verbally.

Real-World Example: Second Life as a Virtual Classroom

One of the earliest and most well-known examples of a virtual world used for education is **Second Life. Second Life** is a **virtual 3D world** where users can create avatars, interact with each other, and explore a vast array of user-created content, from businesses to art galleries to educational institutions. Launched in 2003 by **Linden Lab**, Second Life became a pioneer in bringing virtual spaces to life for educational purposes.

1. **Educational Use in Universities:** Many universities have used **Second Life** as a virtual classroom. Institutions like **Harvard, MIT,** and **University of Phoenix** have created virtual campuses within Second Life, where students can attend classes, visit virtual libraries, and engage in lectures and discussions. Professors can hold office hours, give lectures, and facilitate group discussions, all in a virtual space.

2. **Immersive   Learning:**
In Second Life, students can participate in **immersive learning experiences** that would otherwise be impossible in a traditional classroom. For example, in a virtual archaeology class, students might explore the ruins of ancient civilizations, conduct virtual excavations, and analyze artifacts. This type of learning enhances engagement and comprehension by giving students real-world context and hands-on experience.

3. **Global   Classroom   Access:**
The beauty of Second Life lies in its ability to connect students from around the world. With a virtual campus, students from different countries can attend classes together, participate in group discussions, and collaborate on projects in real time. This fosters a **global learning community**, expanding the educational reach beyond geographical and cultural barriers.

4. **Creative   Expression   and   Learning:**
Second Life also allows for **creative expression**, where students can design and build their own environments, objects, and virtual goods. This fosters innovation and hands-on learning, as students

can explore and develop skills in digital design, architecture, and engineering. Students can create entire educational buildings, virtual exhibitions, and immersive art galleries, which can then be shared with others.

Example in Action:

- **University of Illinois at Urbana-Champaign** has been using Second Life to facilitate virtual medical simulations, where students can practice and simulate complex surgeries in a controlled, safe environment. These virtual simulations allow students to experience medical procedures without the risk or cost associated with real-life practice.

This chapter highlights the **rise of the Metaverse** and its growing role in **education**. With the integration of VR technology, the Metaverse is becoming an immersive space where learning is not confined to traditional tools. Through virtual worlds, social VR, and interactive learning experiences, students can engage with content in more dynamic and memorable ways. The example of **Second Life** as a virtual classroom demonstrates how the Metaverse is already shaping the future of education by breaking geographical barriers, offering immersive learning, and creating a sense of presence in the virtual classroom. As VR continues to evolve, the Metaverse will play an increasingly critical role in the next generation of education.

CHAPTER 7

HOW VR IS RESHAPING CLASSROOM DYNAMICS

Virtual Classrooms: Moving Beyond the Physical Space

The traditional classroom, defined by physical walls, desks, and textbooks, is rapidly evolving into a more flexible, interactive, and immersive space thanks to **Virtual Reality (VR)**. **Virtual classrooms** break free from the limitations of physical infrastructure, enabling both students and teachers to interact in dynamic digital environments. In a virtual classroom, the boundaries of geography and location no longer apply, allowing students from anywhere in the world to participate in the same learning experience.

1. **A New Way of Learning:** Virtual classrooms use VR technology to transport students into immersive, 3D environments where they can engage with the content in real time. These environments are not confined by traditional classroom settings; rather, they can mimic any

setting, from **historic landmarks** to **space explorations** to **science labs**. In this way, VR classrooms provide students with experiential learning opportunities that would be impossible in a typical physical classroom.

2. **Beyond the Four Walls:** Unlike traditional learning, where students are physically bound to the classroom, VR allows them to "travel" to anywhere in the world. Students can virtually visit museums, historical sites, and other places of interest, expanding their learning to new locations, all without leaving their desks. This allows for interactive field trips that bring textbooks to life and offer real-world context for their lessons.

3. **Interactive Learning:** In a virtual classroom, students can participate in hands-on activities that reinforce their learning. Whether it's solving a math puzzle in a 3D environment, conducting experiments in virtual science labs, or exploring virtual ecosystems in biology, VR enables a level of interaction that traditional tools simply cannot. By providing experiences that are both engaging and informative,

VR encourages students to take an active role in their education.

4. **Flexibility in Learning:** Virtual classrooms also provide greater flexibility for **asynchronous learning**. Students can log in at different times, interact with pre-recorded content, and access learning materials whenever they need them. This flexibility allows for a more personalized learning experience that caters to each student's pace, while still offering the chance for live, real-time interaction when needed.

The Teacher's Role in Virtual Reality Learning Environments

While VR can be an incredibly powerful tool in education, the role of the **teacher** remains essential, albeit in a slightly different form. In a virtual reality setting, the teacher's role evolves from being the traditional **lecturer** to more of a **facilitator** and **guide** who steers the learning experience and supports students' interactions in the virtual environment.

1. **Facilitator of Learning:** In a VR classroom, the teacher no longer needs to stand in front of a chalkboard or projector screen. Instead, the teacher's primary role is to facilitate

student engagement in the virtual environment. This means guiding students through various VR experiences, helping them interpret what they encounter, and encouraging exploration. Rather than simply imparting knowledge, the teacher helps students draw connections between what they are experiencing in VR and the concepts they are learning.

2. **Personalized   Instruction:** The ability to track students' interactions within VR environments allows the teacher to offer **personalized feedback** and guidance. Teachers can monitor students' progress, identify areas of struggle, and adjust the virtual lesson plans to meet the individual needs of students. For example, if a student struggles with a certain math problem in a virtual simulation, the teacher can provide tailored support to address the issue in real time.

3. **Creating Collaborative Learning Experiences:** Virtual classrooms foster collaborative learning, where students work together in the VR environment to solve problems, complete tasks, or explore new ideas. Teachers can design group activities within the VR space, encouraging teamwork and social

learning. Teachers act as moderators and mentors, overseeing interactions and guiding students as they collaborate with their peers in the digital world.

4. **Managing Virtual Classrooms:** In a VR classroom, teachers must also manage the technical aspects of the environment. This includes setting up and maintaining the virtual learning space, ensuring that all students have access to the technology, and addressing any technical issues that arise during the lesson. Teachers also ensure that students are safe in the virtual environment, preventing harmful behavior or distractions from affecting the learning experience.

5. **Using Data to Drive Instruction:** VR technology allows teachers to gather **data** on student behavior and performance within the virtual classroom. By analyzing students' actions, the teacher can gain insights into how each student is interacting with the material, what concepts they are struggling with, and where they excel. This data can be used to refine lessons, improve student engagement, and ensure that the learning experience is as effective as possible.

Real-World Example: VR Classrooms and Remote Learning

The rise of **remote learning** during the COVID-19 pandemic highlighted the need for innovative solutions to engage students and bridge the gap left by physical classrooms. While traditional online learning platforms such as Zoom or Google Meet provided a stopgap, VR technology took remote education to the next level by creating immersive environments where students could still engage with content and interact with their peers in meaningful ways.

1. **AltspaceVR – Virtual Classroom Environments:** **AltspaceVR** is one of the most prominent platforms offering virtual event spaces and **virtual classrooms**. Educators have used AltspaceVR to host live lectures, virtual campus tours, and collaborative group projects. Students can participate in these events through VR headsets, where they can interact with other students and teachers, ask questions, and engage in discussions. AltspaceVR's environment allows for a highly interactive experience where students can move around, take notes, and have live conversations as if they were physically in a classroom.

2. **ClassVR – Bringing VR to the Classroom: ClassVR** is a platform designed to integrate VR into the classroom. It's a relatively affordable solution that allows teachers to set up VR experiences for their students. Teachers can design virtual field trips, provide virtual lab experiences, and facilitate collaborative projects. ClassVR also enables teachers to monitor students' progress, ensuring that each student is engaging with the material and benefiting from the VR experience.

3. **Virtual Reality in Higher Education:** In **higher education**, universities are increasingly adopting VR classrooms for remote learning. For instance, **University College London (UCL)** has experimented with VR environments for remote learning, allowing students to attend virtual lectures, participate in seminars, and interact with professors and peers in real time. This helps maintain a sense of connection and engagement, even when students are physically distanced.

4. **Remote Science Labs:** In the realm of **remote science education**, VR is transforming how students conduct experiments. Companies like **Labster** have created **virtual science labs** that allow students to

perform chemistry, biology, and physics experiments from anywhere in the world. These labs simulate real-life scientific procedures and offer a safe, hands-on experience that would be difficult to replicate through traditional remote learning platforms.

This chapter demonstrated how **Virtual Reality (VR) is** reshaping **classroom dynamics** by providing an immersive, interactive, and flexible learning environment. VR allows students to move beyond the limitations of traditional physical classrooms and engage in learning experiences that are dynamic and engaging. As VR continues to evolve, the teacher's role shifts from being a lecturer to a facilitator of personalized, collaborative learning. The integration of VR in **remote learning** environments, as seen with platforms like AltspaceVR and ClassVR, highlights how VR can bridge the gap between physical and online education, providing students with meaningful, engaging, and interactive learning experiences no matter where they are. As VR technology matures, its potential to revolutionize the way we learn and teach will only grow.

CHAPTER 8

IMMERSIVE LEARNING IN K-12 EDUCATION

How VR is Changing Elementary and High School Learning

Virtual Reality (VR) is having a profound impact on **K-12 education**, transforming the way students in elementary and high schools engage with their lessons. Traditionally, students have learned through textbooks, lectures, and visual aids, often limiting their engagement to what they can read or see in 2D. VR, however, introduces a whole new dimension of learning by immersing students in 3D environments, allowing them to interact with the content in ways that weren't previously possible.

1. **Engagement Through Immersion:** In VR, students experience **active, hands-on learning** that deepens their understanding of concepts. For example, instead of simply reading about the solar system, students can "travel" through space, observing planets and stars up close. This immersive approach

increases student engagement by transforming abstract concepts into real, tangible experiences.

2. **Learning Through Exploration:** VR also enables students to **explore virtual environments** that would be impossible or impractical to visit in real life. A student studying marine biology might explore the Great Barrier Reef in VR, observing the diverse marine life and learning about ocean ecosystems firsthand. This type of exploratory learning helps students understand concepts through visual and experiential means, making the material more memorable.

3. **Personalized and Adaptive Learning:** VR in K-12 education allows for **personalized learning** experiences. With VR technology, students can progress at their own pace, revisit difficult concepts, and explore topics they are interested in. For instance, a student struggling with a specific science topic can engage in VR simulations repeatedly until they understand the concept. This level of individualized learning is not always possible in traditional classrooms, where the teacher must address the needs of an entire group.

4. **Promoting Active Participation:** One of the key aspects of VR is its ability to **encourage active participation**. In a traditional classroom, students often absorb information passively. VR, on the other hand, requires students to interact, experiment, and solve problems. This active engagement enhances learning and helps students develop critical thinking and problem-solving skills.

5. **Collaboration in Virtual Spaces:** VR also fosters collaboration among students. In virtual environments, students can work together on projects, share ideas, and solve challenges in real time. This collaborative learning is beneficial for developing teamwork and communication skills, which are crucial for success in both academic and professional settings.

Subject-Specific Applications: Science, History, and Literature

The flexibility and immersive nature of VR allow for its application across a wide range of subjects in **elementary and high school education**, including **science, history, and literature**. Each subject benefits from the unique capabilities of VR to bring concepts to life in interactive and engaging ways.

73

1. **Science:** VR is particularly impactful in the **science** classroom, where students can interact with complex concepts and systems. Instead of learning about the human circulatory system from a textbook, students can explore a **3D model of the human body** in virtual reality, observing how blood flows through the heart, veins, and arteries. Similarly, in **chemistry**, students can mix virtual chemicals and observe reactions in a safe and controlled environment.

   Example Applications:

   o Virtual dissection of animals or human organs.

   o Exploring the deep ocean or the surface of Mars in a **virtual field trip**.

   o Understanding the laws of physics by experimenting with gravity, motion, and forces in virtual simulations.

2. **History: History** education often involves learning about events, places, and people from the past, which can be challenging for students to fully grasp through textbooks alone. VR can take students on **virtual historical tours**, where they can walk through

ancient cities, witness key events, and interact with historical figures. For example, students studying **ancient Egypt** can virtually visit the pyramids, learning about the architecture and culture of the time.

Example Applications:

o Visiting **ancient Rome** or **medieval castles** to observe the architecture and lifestyle.

o Participating in **virtual historical reenactments**, such as the signing of the Declaration of Independence or battles from the Civil War.

o Walking through **historical landmarks**, like the Great Wall of China, as part of a geography lesson.

3. **Literature:** VR is also transforming how **literature** is taught by immersing students in the worlds of the stories they read. Rather than simply analyzing texts from the outside, students can step into the scenes described in the books. In **English literature**, for instance, students studying **Shakespeare** might "visit" the Globe Theatre and experience a play in a way that connects them more deeply with the

material. Similarly, students reading **Homer's Iliad** or **The Adventures of Huckleberry Finn** can explore the environments and settings of the books in virtual space.

Example Applications:

- o Walking through the streets of **Victorian London** during a Dickens novel study.
- o Stepping into the world of **Narnia** in a VR adaptation of C.S. Lewis' stories.
- o Exploring the setting of **The Great Gatsby** and interacting with characters to understand the socio-economic context better.

Real-World Example: VR Field Trips and Interactive Learning

One of the most exciting aspects of VR in K-12 education is its ability to provide **virtual field trips** and **interactive learning** experiences. Virtual field trips allow students to visit places they may never have the opportunity to see in real life, offering them the chance to explore diverse ecosystems, historical landmarks, or even distant planets— all from their classroom.

1. **Virtual Field Trips:** Thanks to VR, students can "travel" to places like the **Amazon Rainforest**, **Mount Everest**, or the **Great Barrier Reef**, all while sitting in their classroom. These virtual trips offer more than just a static view; they allow students to interact with their surroundings, observe wildlife, and even engage in activities like collecting samples or taking measurements.

   Example Applications:

   o A **virtual tour** of the **Pyramids of Giza** for students studying ancient civilizations.

   o A **tour** of the **International Space Station** for students learning about space exploration.

   o Exploring the **Savannah** of Africa to study animals and ecosystems in a geography lesson.

2. **Interactive Learning in Science: VR science labs** provide students with opportunities to perform experiments in a **safe, controlled environment**. For example, students can conduct chemistry experiments, create biological specimens, or even build complex physics machines—all in virtual reality. These experiences provide a more dynamic

and engaging way to learn compared to traditional hands-on methods, where students may be limited by equipment availability, safety concerns, or time constraints.

Real-World Example:

- o **Labster** offers virtual science labs for K-12 students, where they can conduct realistic experiments and simulations. This not only enhances learning but also ensures that students get to experience science at a deeper level, understanding concepts that are often hard to visualize or simulate in the real world.

3. **Interactive Storytelling in Literature:** In literature classes, VR enables **interactive storytelling**, where students become part of the narrative. For instance, while reading **The Odyssey**, students can participate in the hero's journey, making choices that affect the storyline and interacting with the characters. This form of **interactive learning** brings literature to life, making students more connected to the material and enhancing their understanding of the narrative.

Real-World Example:

- o **VR education platforms like ENGAGE** offer interactive storytelling sessions where students can explore key scenes from literature, such as **Shakespeare's Hamlet**, and participate in the play's events, deepening their understanding of themes, characters, and settings.

This chapter has demonstrated the transformative role of VR in **K-12 education**, highlighting how it enhances learning through immersive experiences. By moving beyond the constraints of physical classrooms and textbooks, VR offers **interactive, subject-specific applications** that bring science, history, and literature to life. Real-world examples of **virtual field trips** and **interactive learning** highlight how VR is making education more engaging, dynamic, and accessible for students across the world. As VR continues to evolve, its potential to revolutionize K-12 education will only grow, providing students with opportunities to learn in ways that were once unimaginable.

CHAPTER 9

VR FOR HIGHER EDUCATION

Virtual Campuses and Simulated University Experiences

In the rapidly evolving world of higher education, **Virtual Reality (VR)** is emerging as a transformative tool for both teaching and learning. One of the most innovative applications of VR in universities is the creation of **virtual campuses**—immersive, 3D digital environments that replicate real-world university settings. These campuses provide a unique, engaging way for students to experience university life without being physically present.

1. **Virtual Campuses:** A **virtual campus** allows students to attend classes, visit campus buildings, interact with instructors and peers, and even explore campus grounds—all within a VR environment. For students attending online universities or distance learning programs, a virtual campus can bridge the gap between the isolation of remote learning and the vibrant, community-driven experience of a traditional university campus.

Virtual campuses are equipped with various educational tools, such as **lecture halls**, **libraries**, and **student unions**—all modeled in 3D. Students can navigate through these spaces, attend events, participate in clubs, and even engage in social activities, just as they would in a physical campus environment.

2. **Simulated University Experiences:** VR can also provide **simulated university experiences** where students can practice real-world skills and participate in interactive learning activities. For example, medical students can simulate surgeries, engineering students can test their designs in virtual labs, and business students can participate in virtual simulations of corporate environments. These simulations create safe, controlled spaces where students can practice and learn without real-world consequences, gaining valuable hands-on experience.

This is especially helpful for disciplines where real-life experience is necessary but may not be feasible due to cost, safety, or accessibility constraints. Virtual campuses, equipped with these simulations, offer an immersive learning environment where students can prepare for real-life challenges in their respective fields.

3. **Access for Global Students:** Another advantage of virtual campuses is that they provide **global access** to university resources and social experiences. Students who cannot afford to travel, who live in remote areas, or who face mobility challenges can participate in university life without the geographical or physical barriers. VR campuses provide equitable access to higher education by allowing students to attend lectures, network with peers, and engage in extracurricular activities, regardless of location.

Remote Learning with VR: How Universities are Adapting

The COVID-19 pandemic has accelerated the adoption of **remote learning**, and many universities have turned to VR to make this shift more effective and engaging. While traditional online learning relies on video lectures, discussion boards, and written assignments, VR allows for more **interactive and immersive experiences** that mimic in-person learning environments.

1. **Enhanced Learning Environments:** Traditional online learning platforms often feel disconnected, with students attending lectures through video conferencing tools like Zoom. VR, however, provides a much more interactive experience by immersing students in a virtual classroom. In a VR classroom, students can **sit next to each other**, listen to a lecture, raise their hands to ask questions, and even break into small groups for discussions—much like in a physical classroom.

2. **Simulating Real-World Interactions:** In remote learning scenarios, VR offers an opportunity to **simulate real-world interactions** that are difficult to replicate online. For example, in a virtual business course, students can participate in mock **negotiations**, **business meetings**, or **sales pitches**, gaining hands-on experience without the need for physical presence. VR can even be used to simulate **global business environments**, where students from around the world can interact, collaborate, and work on projects in real time, providing them with practical experience in a global context.

3. **Engagement and Motivation:** One of the key challenges of remote learning is maintaining student

engagement. VR helps tackle this issue by creating **dynamic and immersive content** that actively engages students. Virtual environments are highly interactive, requiring students to move, explore, and participate in various tasks, which increases motivation and retention. Additionally, the novelty of VR helps capture students' attention, making learning feel less like a chore and more like an experience.

4. **Real-Time Feedback:** VR systems in universities can also provide real-time **feedback and assessment** on student performance. Whether it's a lab simulation or a virtual field trip, instructors can monitor students' actions within the virtual environment and provide immediate guidance or corrections. This interactive feedback loop ensures that students stay on track and receive support when needed, even when learning remotely.

5. **Hybrid Learning Opportunities:** Some universities are combining **traditional in-person learning** with VR technology, creating **hybrid learning environments**. In these environments, students attend physical classes for some subjects, while engaging in VR-based lessons for others. This

blend of in-person and virtual learning allows universities to offer the best of both worlds, using VR for subjects that benefit from immersive environments, such as engineering, architecture, medicine, and the arts.

Real-World Example: Virtual University Campuses During the COVID-19 Pandemic

The **COVID-19 pandemic** forced universities worldwide to adapt quickly to remote learning. As a result, many institutions turned to VR to maintain student engagement and provide a more immersive learning experience. Here are a few examples of how VR has been used in higher education during the pandemic:

1. **University of Illinois Virtual Campus:** The University of Illinois at Urbana-Champaign was one of the first universities to experiment with a **virtual campus** for remote learning during the pandemic. They used VR to create a **virtual campus experience** where students could attend classes, meet with professors, and collaborate with peers in a fully immersive, 3D environment. The virtual campus allowed students to interact with one

another, participate in group activities, and engage with the university's resources, despite the restrictions of physical distancing.

2. **Virtual Reality at the University of Oxford:** At the University of Oxford, the **Oxford Virtual Campus** was launched as part of their response to the pandemic. This VR environment allowed students to attend lectures and tutorials, participate in discussions, and interact with academic staff, all in a virtual space. The platform replicated the university's real-world campus layout, complete with libraries, lecture halls, and social areas. This virtual experience provided students with a sense of normalcy and continuity during a time when they could not physically attend classes.

3. **The University of Maryland and the VR Lecture Hall:** The University of Maryland introduced **VR lecture halls** to help students engage with their classes remotely. In these virtual lecture halls, students could watch live lectures in 360-degree environments, participate in group activities, and interact with classmates and professors in real time. This platform was particularly effective for **STEM**

courses, where complex concepts could be better understood through 3D simulations and virtual labs.

4. **The Rise of VR for Medical Education: Medical schools** around the world also adapted VR for remote learning during the pandemic. Virtual simulations allowed medical students to practice **surgical procedures**, **diagnostic techniques**, and **patient interactions** in a controlled, immersive environment. VR provided a way for students to continue their education and practice real-world skills without the need for physical access to medical facilities.

This chapter has explored how **Virtual Reality (VR)** is reshaping **higher education**, from virtual campuses to **remote learning** environments. Through immersive, interactive, and engaging virtual spaces, VR is enabling universities to offer students a more dynamic, global, and flexible learning experience. The rise of **virtual university campuses** and **VR-enabled education** during the COVID-19 pandemic has demonstrated the potential of VR in overcoming challenges faced by remote learning, providing students with the tools they need to continue their education despite external obstacles. As VR technology continues to evolve, its impact on higher education will only expand, offering new possibilities for immersive learning, global collaboration, and innovative teaching methods.

CHAPTER 10

VR IN VOCATIONAL AND SKILLS TRAINING

VR for Career-Specific Education and Skill Acquisition

Virtual Reality (VR) has become a powerful tool in **vocational and skills training**, providing students and professionals with the ability to acquire hands-on experience in their respective fields without the risks or costs associated with real-world practice. In fields such as **engineering**, **medicine**, **construction**, and **aviation**, VR is revolutionizing how individuals learn and refine their skills, offering more **interactive** and **immersive** training experiences than traditional methods.

1. **Simulated Real-World Experience:** Career-specific training often requires practice in complex or high-stakes environments, where making mistakes can have serious consequences. With VR, trainees can practice in a **simulated environment** that mirrors real-life scenarios, allowing them to gain proficiency and confidence before performing tasks in the real world. VR offers an opportunity to

repeatedly practice scenarios, making it ideal for fields where **repetition and mastery** are key.

2. **Hands-On Training in a Virtual Space:** Vocational training typically involves practical, hands-on work. With VR, students can simulate this practical experience without the need for costly materials, physical space, or direct supervision. For example, a **mechanical engineering student** can assemble machines, test components, and troubleshoot in a virtual workshop. Similarly, an **IT technician** can practice diagnosing network issues, troubleshooting software, or assembling computer hardware in a digital environment.

3. **Remote Access to Training:** VR also makes vocational training more accessible to individuals who may be geographically distant from training centers or institutions. For example, a student in a rural area can participate in the same hands-on training as someone in a major city, reducing barriers to entry and providing more equitable access to career-specific education.

4. **Cost-Effectiveness and Scalability:** Traditional vocational training often requires substantial resources—whether it's tools, materials, or human

instructors. VR eliminates many of these costs by allowing for scalable training solutions that can be accessed remotely. Additionally, VR programs can be **customized** to suit the specific needs of various industries, ensuring that training remains up-to-date with current best practices and technologies.

5. **Soft Skills Training:** VR is also beneficial for developing **soft skills** that are essential for many careers, such as **communication, problem-solving**, and **leadership**. For instance, a **customer service representative** can practice handling difficult customers in a virtual environment, while a **manager** can engage in leadership scenarios that help them develop conflict resolution or decision-making skills.

Training in High-Risk Environments: Safety Simulations

One of the most significant benefits of VR in vocational and skills training is its ability to provide **safety simulations** for high-risk environments. Certain careers—such as those in the **military, construction, firefighting**, and **medicine**— involve potentially dangerous situations, where safety is paramount. VR allows professionals to train in these environments without exposure to actual danger, making it a **vital tool for safety** and risk management.

1. **Simulating Dangerous Scenarios:** VR offers the ability to simulate dangerous situations in a controlled, virtual space. For example, **firefighters** can experience the heat and smoke of a burning building, learning how to respond to fires without actually being exposed to fire-related risks. **Construction workers** can practice working at heights or handling heavy equipment in a virtual construction site, learning proper safety protocols before engaging in real-world tasks.

2. **Emergency Response Training:** In fields such as **emergency medicine**, **police**, and **firefighting**, VR allows trainees to practice responding to high-pressure situations. These environments mimic real-life emergencies, such as medical triage, natural disasters, or accident scenes. Students can practice making life-saving decisions, communicating with teammates, and implementing emergency protocols in a virtual setting.

VR's ability to simulate **real-world urgency** in these training environments enhances preparedness, as trainees can repeatedly experience and respond to a variety of scenarios. This prepares them to handle real-life crises more effectively.

3. **Reducing Risk and Cost:** Safety training can be expensive and dangerous if conducted in the real world. By using VR simulations, institutions can eliminate the need for costly physical setups, hazardous materials, or live demonstrations. Moreover, VR training ensures that students are better prepared and less likely to make mistakes in high-risk environments.

4. **Virtual Dangerous Equipment Handling:** VR allows trainees to interact with **dangerous equipment** in a safe, virtual space. For example, oil rig workers, nuclear technicians, and factory employees can practice operating large, complex machinery without the risks associated with real-world operations. They can get a feel for the equipment, understand how it works, and become familiar with emergency shutdown procedures—all in a risk-free environment.

5. **Accident Reconstruction for Training:** In industries like law enforcement, emergency response, and even automotive engineering, VR can

be used to **reconstruct accidents** or incidents. VR enables trainees to examine accident scenes in 3D, understanding the chain of events that led to an incident. For example, **accident reconstruction specialists** can study virtual simulations of crashes, which helps them investigate causes, train emergency response teams, and provide insight into accident prevention.

Real-World Example: VR Training for Healthcare Professionals

The **healthcare** industry is one of the most prominent fields where VR is making an impact, particularly in medical education and training. VR allows healthcare professionals to practice complex procedures, engage in simulations of medical scenarios, and refine their skills without putting patients at risk. This has proven to be incredibly valuable in preparing future doctors, nurses, surgeons, and other healthcare workers for high-pressure situations.

1. **Medical Simulations:** VR has become a game-changer for medical schools, offering **virtual surgeries**, diagnostic simulations, and patient care scenarios. Students can practice everything from

surgical procedures to **patient interaction** in a virtual setting, receiving real-time feedback as they work. This gives students the ability to build their **practical skills** in a controlled, safe, and repeatable environment.

Example:

- o **Osso VR** is a platform used in medical training that allows healthcare professionals to practice surgical techniques on virtual patients. The platform offers a wide range of simulations, including **orthopedic** and **neurosurgical procedures**, enabling students to learn techniques in a risk-free environment. These simulations are designed to replicate real-life surgeries as closely as possible, providing valuable experience before entering the operating room.

2. **Virtual Patient Interaction:** VR is also used to simulate interactions with **virtual patients**, giving healthcare students the opportunity to practice diagnosing symptoms, taking patient histories, and performing medical procedures. These simulations can replicate the **emotional and psychological**

95

aspects of patient care, helping students develop empathy and communication skills.

Example:

- o **VIRTUAL MEDICAL** is a VR platform that simulates real-world medical scenarios, allowing students to interact with virtual patients. These patients may present with a range of symptoms, requiring students to make diagnoses and administer treatments. By interacting with these virtual patients, healthcare professionals can build confidence in patient care before applying their skills in real-world settings.

3. **Simulated Medical Emergencies:** In high-pressure fields such as **emergency medicine**, VR is used to simulate medical emergencies like cardiac arrests, trauma care, and respiratory distress. Healthcare professionals can practice delivering **life-saving interventions**, managing medical crises, and responding to complex scenarios, all in a virtual setting. These simulations help professionals learn how to act quickly and effectively, making them better prepared for real emergencies.

4. **Training for High-Risk Procedures:** Complex and high-risk procedures, such as **brain surgeries** or **heart transplants**, can be difficult and dangerous to practice in real life. VR allows students to perform these procedures in a safe, risk-free environment where they can familiarize themselves with the steps involved, practice techniques, and build confidence before performing surgery on a real patient.

This chapter has highlighted how **VR is reshaping vocational and skills training**, offering career-specific education in immersive, interactive environments. Through **safety simulations**, **real-world procedural practice**, and **simulated environments**, VR offers students and professionals the chance to build skills, gain experience, and refine techniques in a controlled and repeatable space. **VR training for healthcare professionals**, in particular, demonstrates the potential for VR to revolutionize medical education, allowing future doctors, surgeons, and emergency responders to practice life-saving procedures without the risks of real-world training. As VR technology continues to advance, its applications in vocational and skills training will only expand, offering even more opportunities for students to gain valuable hands-on experience across various industries.

CHAPTER 11

COLLABORATIVE LEARNING IN THE METAVERSE

Virtual Group Work and Collaboration in VR Spaces

One of the most transformative aspects of the Metaverse is its ability to bring together individuals in **virtual spaces** to collaborate and work together in ways that were previously impossible. **Virtual reality (VR)** facilitates **collaborative learning** by allowing students to engage in group work, problem-solving tasks, and creative projects within immersive virtual environments.

1. **Creating Virtual Classrooms for Collaboration:** In VR, the concept of the **virtual classroom** extends beyond a simple video call or discussion forum. These environments are rich, 3D spaces where students can come together, share ideas, and work collaboratively. Virtual classrooms can include a wide range of tools, such as **whiteboards**, **interactive objects**, **video feeds**, and **real-time**

99

collaboration spaces that make it easier for students to share their work, discuss ideas, and brainstorm solutions.

2. **Shared Virtual Workspaces:** Virtual workspaces in VR are designed to foster **group work and interaction**. Students can work together in **3D spaces** where they can manipulate objects, write on virtual whiteboards, or even **build projects** collaboratively. These shared spaces allow participants to feel like they are physically present in the same location, which enhances communication and engagement.

3. **Global Collaboration:** VR removes geographical boundaries, enabling students from different parts of the world to collaborate seamlessly in real-time. This creates opportunities for **global teamwork**, where individuals from diverse cultural backgrounds can share perspectives, contribute unique ideas, and solve problems together. For instance, students in the U.S. and India can participate in the same virtual project, engage in cross-cultural exchanges, and solve complex challenges, all while working in the same VR space.

4. **Immersive Communication Tools:** In VR spaces, communication isn't limited to voice or text; it includes **gestures**, **body language**, and **non-verbal cues**, which are crucial for effective collaboration. For example, students can point to objects, draw on virtual surfaces, and express themselves through their avatars. These non-verbal communication methods mimic face-to-face interactions, enhancing the overall collaboration experience.

How VR Encourages Teamwork and Problem-Solving Skills

VR not only promotes collaboration but also fosters the development of **teamwork** and **problem-solving skills**. The nature of VR environments encourages students to work together toward common goals, tackle challenges, and solve problems in creative ways.

1. **Simulating Real-World Challenges:** VR allows educators to create **real-world simulations** in which students must work together to solve problems. For example, students in a **VR medical training simulation

A network error occurred. Please check your connection and try again. If this issue persists please contact us through our help center at help.openai.com.

CHAPTER 12

PERSONALIZED LEARNING EXPERIENCES WITH VR

How VR Can Adapt to Individual Learning Styles

One of the greatest strengths of **Virtual Reality (VR)** in education is its ability to **personalize learning experiences** to meet the unique needs of each student. Traditional education systems often rely on a one-size-fits-all approach, where all students must learn the same material in the same way, regardless of their individual learning preferences, strengths, or weaknesses. VR, however, provides a dynamic and flexible environment that can adapt to various **learning styles**—ensuring that every student receives the support and engagement they need.

1. **Visual**   **Learners:**
   Visual learners thrive when they can see information presented in graphical or spatial formats. VR allows these learners to interact with **3D visuals**, **virtual simulations**, and **interactive graphics** that help

them better understand complex concepts. For example, in a **virtual anatomy lesson**, visual learners can explore 3D models of the human body, zooming in to see the heart, lungs, and organs from every angle. This hands-on visual interaction makes abstract concepts more concrete.

2. **Auditory** **Learners:**

For auditory learners, VR can provide immersive experiences that incorporate sound and narration. In a **virtual history class**, for instance, students can listen to historical figures narrating events, with **background sounds** creating a more vivid, realistic experience. By combining auditory stimuli with visual elements, VR caters to those who learn best through listening and hearing.

3. **Kinesthetic** **Learners:**

Kinesthetic learners—who learn best through hands-on activities and physical movement—benefit from VR's interactive nature. VR enables these students to engage physically with the learning material. For instance, in a **virtual science lab**, students can mix chemicals, observe reactions, and interact with lab equipment. This **hands-on experience** helps kinesthetic learners build muscle memory and deepen their understanding by doing rather than just observing.

4. **Adaptive Learning Paths:** VR systems can also be designed to **adapt** to a student's progress and needs. For instance, if a student excels in a particular area, the VR system can present more complex scenarios or tasks, while providing additional support for students who need extra assistance. This **adaptive learning** ensures that every student is working at a level that challenges them appropriately, without overwhelming or under-stimulating them.

5. **Learning   Pacing:** One of the most significant advantages of VR is that it allows students to learn at their own pace. In traditional classrooms, students often have to move at the speed of the lesson or course. With VR, however, students can revisit lessons, take breaks, or move ahead if they grasp the material quickly. This **self-paced learning** is particularly valuable for students with different learning speeds or those who need to spend additional time on certain concepts.

Data-Driven Education: Monitoring Progress in Real-Time

Another powerful aspect of **VR in education** is its ability to **collect and analyze data** in real-time, providing valuable insights into a student's progress and performance. This data-driven approach enhances the learning experience by enabling both instructors and students to monitor progress, adjust learning paths, and identify areas for improvement.

1. **Real-Time Tracking of Progress:** VR systems are equipped with sensors and tracking mechanisms that monitor a student's **engagement**, **interaction**, and **performance**. For instance, in a virtual math lesson, the system can track how long a student spends on a particular problem, how they solve it, and whether they make progress over time. This data helps teachers understand which students need more support or which concepts require additional focus.

2. **Personalized Feedback:** Based on the data gathered, VR platforms can deliver **personalized feedback** to students. For example, if a student struggles to grasp a particular concept or make progress in a simulation, the system can provide additional hints, visual cues, or simplify tasks until the student gains confidence. This **immediate**

feedback loop ensures that students don't fall behind and can address areas of difficulty as they arise.

3. **Assessment and Reporting:** Traditional assessments like tests and quizzes may not always capture a student's true understanding or progress. VR, on the other hand, can assess a student's performance through **interactive simulations** and tasks that require them to apply what they've learned. For example, in a **virtual medical training program**, a student's ability to perform surgery or diagnose a condition can be assessed in real-time, with detailed reports generated based on their actions, decisions, and outcomes.

4. **Data Visualization for Teachers:** Teachers can use the data generated by VR systems to **visualize student progress** and tailor instruction accordingly. For instance, if a student is struggling with a particular task, the teacher can receive a report highlighting the areas where the student needs more help. This data can be used to inform instructional strategies, ensuring that each student receives the support they need in real-time.

5. **Tracking Learning Over Time:** Data from VR platforms can be stored and analyzed over time,

providing a long-term view of a student's development. This allows for **longitudinal tracking**, which can be invaluable for understanding how a student is progressing, identifying trends, and adjusting the learning experience to accommodate their evolving needs.

Real-World Example: Personalized Medical Training with VR Simulations

One of the most impactful applications of **personalized learning with VR** is in **medical education**. Medical training requires hands-on practice and the development of complex skills that must be perfected over time. VR simulations provide medical students with the opportunity to practice these skills in a safe, controlled, and repeatable environment.

1. **Simulating Complex Medical Procedures:** Medical students use VR to **perform virtual surgeries**, practice diagnostics, and experience medical procedures in a way that is personalized to their skill level. For example, in a **virtual surgery simulation**, students can practice performing **knee replacements**, **heart surgeries**, or **emergency trauma care**. The simulation adapts to their actions,

providing **real-time feedback** on their technique, precision, and decision-making.

Personalized Training Paths: VR systems can be set up to track a student's proficiency with different procedures. If a student struggles with a particular aspect of surgery, such as suturing or tissue handling, the VR system can provide additional practice scenarios that focus on that specific skill. This ensures that students have ample opportunity to **refine their technique** before performing real surgeries.

2. **Real-World Example: Osso VR Osso VR** is a leading VR-based surgical training platform used by medical professionals to practice various **surgical procedures** in a risk-free environment. The platform provides a **real-time analysis** of the trainee's performance, including their accuracy and time management during a procedure. Based on this data, Osso VR can **personalize the learning experience**, offering targeted exercises and simulations to help the student improve.

3. **Emergency Response and Diagnostics Training:** VR is also used in **emergency medical training**,

where students can practice handling medical crises such as **cardiac arrest** or **severe trauma**. By using VR simulations, students can face high-pressure scenarios in which they must make quick decisions, manage resources, and deliver care. These scenarios are tailored to each student's skill level, allowing for progressively more complex simulations as their abilities improve.

4. **Patient Interaction and Communication Skills:** In addition to technical skills, VR can help medical students develop **communication skills** when interacting with patients. By using **virtual patients**, students can practice discussing diagnoses, delivering bad news, or answering patient questions. These simulations can be personalized based on the student's progress, helping them improve their bedside manner and patient communication skills.

This chapter has illustrated how **VR creates personalized learning experiences** by adapting to different learning styles and providing real-time data on student progress. In fields like medicine, VR enables **individualized skill development**, from **surgical simulations** to **patient**

communication. The ability to provide **immediate feedback, personalized training paths**, and **real-time monitoring** makes VR an invaluable tool in both academic and professional settings. As VR technology continues to advance, the potential for personalized learning will only expand, making education more accessible, effective, and tailored to the needs of each student.

CHAPTER 13

OVERCOMING LEARNING BARRIERS WITH VR

Accessibility and Inclusivity in Virtual Learning

One of the most significant advantages of **Virtual Reality (VR)** in education is its ability to make learning more **accessible** and **inclusive**. Traditional education systems often face barriers related to physical space, ability, language, and resources. However, VR has the potential to break down these barriers by providing **equal opportunities** for all students, regardless of their personal circumstances.

1. **Accessibility for Students with Disabilities:** VR provides unique solutions for students with disabilities, allowing them to engage with the learning material in ways that may not be possible in traditional classrooms. For instance, students with **visual impairments** can benefit from VR environments that offer audio-based feedback or **haptic technology** that conveys information through

touch or vibration. Similarly, **hearing-impaired students** can access real-time subtitles or sign language interpreters within virtual environments.

For students with **physical disabilities**, VR can simulate physical experiences such as **lab experiments**, **field trips**, or even **sports activities**, enabling them to participate in educational experiences that they may otherwise miss due to mobility issues. Additionally, students with **learning disabilities** can benefit from customized learning paths within VR environments that adapt to their individual learning speed and style.

2. **Language and Cultural Inclusivity:** VR can help bridge language barriers by offering immersive, **multi-lingual environments** where students can learn in their native language or practice a second language. For instance, a student studying **English as a second language** can enter a virtual world where they interact with native speakers and engage in real-time conversations, helping them improve their language skills through natural immersion.

VR also creates opportunities for students to experience other cultures firsthand. In a **history or geography lesson**, students can virtually visit different countries, experience cultural festivals, and interact with avatars representing people from diverse backgrounds. This fosters **cultural awareness** and helps students better understand and appreciate global diversity.

3. **Assistive Technologies in VR:** VR platforms are increasingly incorporating **assistive technologies** to support students with specific learning needs. These technologies include tools like **speech-to-text**, **customizable user interfaces**, and **adaptive controllers** that allow students with physical disabilities to engage with VR content in a manner suited to their abilities. By providing these tools, VR ensures that every student has an opportunity to succeed in a virtual learning environment.

Overcoming Geographic and Financial Barriers

In addition to improving accessibility for students with disabilities, VR also helps overcome **geographic** and **financial barriers** that often limit educational opportunities.

114

In traditional education systems, students in **remote or rural areas** often have limited access to high-quality educational resources, teachers, and extracurricular activities. Similarly, **financial constraints** can prevent students from attending prestigious institutions or accessing specialized learning materials. VR helps level the playing field by bringing world-class education and resources to anyone with access to the technology.

1. **Breaking Geographical Barriers:** One of the key benefits of VR in education is its ability to provide **global access** to educational content and experiences. Students living in remote or underserved areas, where access to high-quality education is limited, can now virtually attend classes, participate in virtual field trips, and collaborate with peers from around the world.

   For example, students in rural areas can take **virtual courses** from prestigious universities or engage in **online collaborative projects** with peers from other countries. With VR, students are no longer restricted by their geographic location, allowing them to explore learning opportunities that might otherwise be out of reach.

115

2. **Affordable Education: VR education** also addresses the issue of financial accessibility. Traditionally, students have had to pay high tuition fees for quality education, along with the costs of textbooks, equipment, and on-campus housing. VR, however, can provide immersive learning experiences at a fraction of the cost. For instance, instead of traveling to another city to take a specialized course, students can attend virtual **workshops**, **seminars**, or **masterclasses** remotely, saving on travel and accommodation expenses.

In addition, VR reduces the need for expensive physical resources. Virtual simulations allow students to conduct experiments or build projects without the need for costly materials, reducing both the overall cost of education and the environmental impact. For example, a **virtual chemistry lab** allows students to perform experiments safely and affordably without requiring expensive chemicals or lab equipment.

3. **Remote Learning for Underfunded Schools:** VR also offers a cost-effective solution for schools in underfunded areas. Many schools, especially those in

low-income neighborhoods, lack the financial resources to provide students with the tools, infrastructure, and teaching materials they need. By adopting VR technology, these schools can provide their students with immersive educational experiences without the need for extensive budgets.

Example: A school in an underprivileged area might not have the funds to set up a physical science lab, but with VR, students can access **virtual science experiments**, explore biology in 3D, and participate in virtual **geography field trips**. This helps bridge the **educational divide**, offering the same opportunities to all students, regardless of their socio-economic status.

Real-World Example: VR for Students in Remote Areas

The power of VR to overcome geographic and financial barriers has been proven in several real-world applications, especially in remote and underserved communities. Here are a few examples:

1. **VR Field Trips for Rural Schools:** Many rural schools face challenges when it comes to taking

students on educational field trips. The distance, cost, and logistical challenges can prevent students from experiencing hands-on learning in museums, historical landmarks, or natural environments. VR field trips, however, have allowed students to "travel" to places like the **Grand Canyon, museums in Paris**, or **the pyramids of Egypt**—all without leaving their classroom. For example, **Google Expeditions**, a platform designed for immersive virtual field trips, offers students in remote schools the chance to visit these important locations in an engaging and interactive way.

2. **Bringing Education to Remote Islands in the Pacific:** In some remote islands of the Pacific, students face limited access to educational resources and expert instructors. However, programs like **VR STEM education initiatives** are helping bring **science education** to these regions by providing access to virtual classrooms and laboratories. By using **virtual labs**, students can engage in science experiments that are difficult or impossible to conduct in their local schools due to resource limitations.

3. **Remote Medical Training for Rural Healthcare Workers:** In rural and underserved regions, medical professionals often face a lack of access to advanced training opportunities. VR is changing that by providing **virtual medical training** to healthcare workers in remote areas. For example, **VRHealth** offers virtual training programs for doctors and nurses in rural Africa, where healthcare workers can practice medical procedures and surgeries virtually. This training improves their skills, allowing them to provide better care to patients in areas with limited medical resources.

4. **VR in Refugee Education:** In conflict zones and refugee camps, access to education is often limited or non-existent. VR has been used in **refugee camps** to provide children with access to **learning resources** and virtual classrooms. By using VR headsets, children in these camps can attend classes, learn mathematics, language skills, and even participate in virtual arts programs. This provides a sense of normalcy and continuity in education for students who might otherwise be left behind due to their difficult circumstances.

This chapter has explored how **Virtual Reality (VR) is overcoming learning barriers** by increasing **accessibility** and **inclusivity**, breaking down **geographic and financial barriers**, and providing **equitable education** for all students. VR offers immense potential to transform education, especially for students in underserved or remote areas, by providing immersive learning experiences that were previously out of reach. Real-world examples, such as **VR field trips** for rural schools, **remote medical training**, and educational opportunities for refugee children, show how VR is helping to bridge the gap in global education. As VR technology continues to evolve, its ability to offer **affordable, accessible, and high-quality education** will grow, ensuring that all students, regardless of their background or location, have the opportunity to learn and succeed.

CHAPTER 14

THE ROLE OF AI IN VR EDUCATION

Artificial Intelligence's Role in Personalizing VR Learning

Artificial Intelligence (AI) is playing an increasingly pivotal role in transforming how education is delivered through Virtual Reality (VR). Together, AI and VR create a **personalized learning experience** that adapts to each student's needs, pace, and learning style, providing **dynamic and responsive educational environments**.

1. **Adaptive Learning Pathways:** AI can **analyze a student's performance** in real-time within a VR environment and adjust the learning content accordingly. For instance, if a student is struggling with a particular concept, the AI can slow down the pace, offer additional resources, or suggest alternative explanations tailored to that student's learning style. Conversely, if a student is excelling,

121

the AI can introduce more complex challenges to keep them engaged.

2. **Intelligent Content Delivery:** AI can **select and deliver content** that aligns with the student's proficiency level. In VR environments, students may experience simulations or interactive tasks, and AI algorithms can detect whether the student is mastering the material or requires extra help. Based on this analysis, AI may alter the difficulty of simulations, change the mode of instruction (e.g., from visual to auditory), or provide additional hints. This dynamic adaptability ensures that the content remains relevant and appropriately challenging.

3. **Personalized Avatars and Interactions:** AI can generate personalized **avatars** for each student, adjusting their responses based on the student's progress and engagement. These avatars can act as **virtual instructors**, providing immediate feedback, answering questions, or offering encouragement during simulations. Over time, these AI-powered avatars can learn from the student's behavior and refine their interactions, enhancing the overall learning experience.

4. **Learning Analytics and Insights:** AI tracks and analyzes vast amounts of data about student interactions within the VR environment. By examining how a student engages with content— whether it's how long they spend on a particular task, how they approach problems, or what types of questions they ask—AI can identify patterns in their learning. This data provides **actionable insights** for both students and educators, allowing for **continuous improvement** and customization of the learning experience.

How AI Helps Improve Student Engagement and Retention

AI doesn't just personalize learning; it also plays a crucial role in improving **student engagement** and **retention** by creating a more **interactive, motivating,** and **rewarding** learning environment. By continuously adapting to students' needs and responding to their progress, AI ensures that the VR learning experience remains **engaging** and **immersive**.

1. **Immediate Feedback and Motivation:** One of the main benefits of AI in VR education is its ability to provide **immediate feedback**. When students make mistakes in traditional educational settings, there's

often a delay before they receive correction, whether through grades or comments from the teacher. In VR environments powered by AI, students receive real-time feedback, allowing them to correct errors, try new approaches, and continue learning without hesitation. This **instant feedback** not only accelerates learning but also increases **motivation**, as students can see their improvement in real-time.

2. **Engagement Through Gamification:** AI in VR can implement **gamified elements** that enhance engagement and make learning fun. For example, AI can create challenges or **missions** within a VR environment, where students earn points, badges, or rewards for completing tasks or solving problems. These game-like features keep students engaged by providing a sense of achievement and progress. The use of **gamification** is especially effective for keeping students motivated, as it turns learning into a rewarding experience.

3. **Emotional Engagement and Support:** AI can be programmed to respond to students' emotional cues, using **emotion recognition** techniques to analyze facial expressions, body language, and voice tone. This allows AI avatars or tutors to **adjust their**

interactions to match the student's emotional state. For example, if a student appears frustrated, the AI can offer encouragement or simplify the task at hand. If a student seems confident and eager, the AI might introduce more advanced content. This emotional responsiveness helps maintain **engagement** and ensures that students feel supported throughout their learning journey.

4. **Predictive Analytics for Retention:** AI-powered systems can use predictive analytics to identify students who may be at risk of disengaging or falling behind. By analyzing factors such as time spent on tasks, frequency of interactions, and progress rates, AI can flag potential issues early on. This allows educators to intervene and offer additional support before the student's disengagement becomes a significant problem, improving overall **retention rates**.

5. **Adaptation to Student Needs:** AI continuously analyzes how a student is performing within the VR environment. If a student is struggling with a specific topic, the AI can suggest alternative learning methods, additional practice tasks, or a change in the type of content presented (e.g., more visuals, fewer

texts). This adaptability ensures that the student remains engaged and does not feel overwhelmed or bored by the material.

Real-World Example: AI-Powered Virtual Tutors and Guides

AI-powered virtual tutors and guides are already being implemented in a variety of educational settings, providing personalized, **real-time support** to students as they navigate VR learning environments. These AI tutors act as mentors, helping students learn at their own pace and providing individualized attention.

1. **AI Virtual Tutors in Language Learning:** One of the most successful applications of AI in VR education is in language learning. Platforms such as **Mondly VR** use AI-powered **virtual tutors** to teach students new languages. These tutors simulate conversations with native speakers, offering real-time corrections and suggestions based on the student's performance. AI tracks the student's vocabulary acquisition, pronunciation, and comprehension, providing personalized feedback and adapting the difficulty level as the student progresses.

2. **AI-Powered Medical Training Simulations:** In **medical education**, AI-powered virtual tutors guide students through complex medical procedures and diagnoses in VR. **Surgical training platforms** like **Osso VR** use AI to simulate surgeries and provide real-time feedback based on the student's actions. The AI tutor can suggest changes to the surgical procedure, point out areas for improvement, and adjust the training to meet the student's skill level. Over time, the AI learns from the student's actions and tailors the training to improve performance and skills in specific areas.

3. **Personalized Support in STEM Education:** In **STEM education**, VR platforms like **Labster** use AI-powered guides to support students conducting virtual science experiments. The AI acts as a virtual lab assistant, helping students set up experiments, explain scientific concepts, and analyze results. Based on the student's progress, the AI tutor may provide additional explanations, suggest relevant experiments, or introduce new topics for exploration. This personalized guidance makes it easier for students to grasp complex scientific concepts while also keeping them engaged in the material.

127

4. **AI-Based Learning Assistants for K-12:** In K-12 education, platforms like **ClassVR** integrate AI-powered **learning assistants** into VR environments to help students navigate educational simulations and virtual lessons. These AI assistants can give instructions, clarify concepts, and assess students' understanding in real-time. They can also offer adaptive learning pathways based on the student's needs, ensuring that each child is challenged appropriately while receiving the support they require.

5. **AI-Driven Career Training Simulations:** VR career training platforms, such as **SkillXR**, incorporate AI-powered guides to help students learn specific career skills. For example, in a virtual construction training environment, the AI tutor can walk students through different tasks, provide on-the-spot feedback, and adapt the simulation's difficulty based on the student's experience level. This level of personalization ensures that students are receiving the most relevant training for their individual needs, preparing them for the workforce more effectively.

This chapter has demonstrated how **Artificial Intelligence (AI)** plays a vital role in **personalizing VR learning experiences**, improving **student engagement**, and enhancing **retention**. AI allows educational systems to adapt to each student's needs, preferences, and pace, creating a more **tailored and effective learning experience**. Through the use of **AI-powered tutors and guides**, students can receive real-time feedback and support, making learning more interactive and individualized. Real-world examples, such as AI-powered medical training, language learning, and STEM education platforms, show how AI and VR can work together to create dynamic, personalized, and engaging educational experiences. As AI continues to advance, its potential to enhance the learning process in virtual environments will only grow, further revolutionizing education across various fields.

CHAPTER 15

THE PSYCHOLOGY OF VR LEARNING

Cognitive Benefits of Learning in Immersive Virtual Environments

Virtual Reality (VR) has proven to be more than just a tool for entertainment—its immersive nature offers numerous **cognitive benefits** that significantly enhance the learning process. Immersion in a VR environment can activate various cognitive processes, making learning more engaging, memorable, and effective.

1. **Enhanced Memory Retention:** Studies show that VR can improve **memory retention** by engaging multiple senses simultaneously. When students are immersed in an interactive environment, they are more likely to remember what they learn. This is due to the brain's tendency to retain information more effectively when it is experienced firsthand, as opposed to simply reading or listening. For example,

students who explore historical sites in VR or engage in virtual science labs are more likely to recall the information because they were actively involved in the experience.

2. **Active Learning and Cognitive Engagement:** In traditional education, students often absorb information passively through lectures or textbooks. However, VR promotes **active learning**, which enhances **cognitive engagement**. In a VR environment, students must navigate challenges, solve problems, and interact with the content. This active involvement strengthens the brain's cognitive connections and promotes deeper learning. For instance, in a VR chemistry lab, students engage with molecules and chemical reactions directly, rather than just reading about them, making the learning process more stimulating and effective.

3. **Spatial Awareness and Problem-Solving:** VR can also improve **spatial awareness**—the ability to understand the positions and relationships between objects in space. When students navigate 3D environments, they develop better spatial reasoning skills, which are crucial for fields like **architecture**, **engineering**, and **medicine**. Additionally, VR

scenarios often require students to engage in **problem-solving** and **critical thinking**, strengthening their decision-making abilities. For example, a student working on a virtual construction project may need to assess the structural integrity of a building, test its components, and troubleshoot issues—all of which require critical thinking and spatial awareness.

4. **Multisensory Learning:** By engaging multiple senses—sight, sound, and even touch (through haptic feedback)—VR creates a **multisensory learning environment** that activates different cognitive pathways in the brain. This multisensory approach makes learning richer and more impactful. For example, a student learning about the human body in VR can not only see anatomical structures but can also interact with them, hear explanations, and feel virtual representations of muscle movements or organ functions.

5. **Improved Focus and Reduced Distractions:** The immersive nature of VR also promotes **focused learning**. In a traditional classroom setting, students may become distracted by their surroundings, technology, or other students. However, in a VR

environment, the student is fully immersed in the virtual world, reducing external distractions and increasing attention and concentration. This focused environment allows for a deeper level of engagement and a more effective learning experience.

The Role of Presence and Emotional Connection in Learning

One of the unique features of VR is its ability to create a sense of **presence**—the feeling of being physically immersed in a virtual space. This sense of presence plays a critical role in learning by enhancing emotional engagement and connection with the content.

1. **Presence and Deep Learning: Presence** refers to the psychological state in which individuals feel as though they are truly "there" in the virtual environment. When students experience presence, they are more likely to **emotionally engage** with the material. This emotional involvement enhances their focus and commitment to learning. For example, when a student participates in a **virtual field trip** to ancient Egypt, they don't just watch a video or read a text; they feel as though they are standing in the ruins, walking through the pyramids, and interacting

133

with historical objects. This strong sense of presence makes the experience more memorable and impactful, increasing the likelihood of long-term retention.

2. **Emotional Connection and Empathy:** VR fosters an emotional connection to the content, which is particularly valuable in fields like **history**, **literature**, **medicine**, and **social sciences**. By immersing students in **empathy-building scenarios**, VR can help them understand the perspectives and experiences of others. For instance, in a **history lesson** on the **Holocaust**, students can experience the events through the eyes of a character, allowing them to gain a deeper, more emotional understanding of the tragedy. This emotional connection promotes **empathy**, which enhances learning and makes students more likely to internalize the lessons being taught.

3. **Simulation of Real-Life Scenarios:** The **emotional impact** of VR learning is heightened when students experience real-life scenarios in a safe and controlled environment. For example, a student training to be a **paramedic** can engage in a **VR emergency simulation**, where they must perform life-saving

procedures under pressure. The emotional intensity of the scenario—such as the urgency of treating a patient in critical condition—helps to develop the student's **emotional intelligence** and **stress management skills**, which are crucial for real-world application.

4. **Immersive Learning for Behavioral Change:** VR also enables **behavioral change** through immersive experiences that allow students to "practice" actions, decisions, and consequences. For instance, VR can be used in **therapy settings** to help students with **social anxiety** or **public speaking** by simulating situations that evoke anxiety, allowing students to practice coping mechanisms in a safe and controlled space. This type of emotional engagement in VR helps students manage their reactions and gain confidence in real-life situations.

Real-World Example: How VR is Used for Trauma Therapy and Learning

One of the most compelling examples of the psychological benefits of VR is its use in **trauma therapy** and emotional learning. VR has been used to help patients confront and work through **traumatic experiences** in a controlled and

135

therapeutic setting, allowing them to **process** and **heal** in ways that were not possible with traditional therapies.

1. **Virtual Reality Exposure Therapy (VRET):** **Virtual Reality Exposure Therapy** (VRET) has been successfully used to treat **Post-Traumatic Stress Disorder** (PTSD) in military veterans, first responders, and victims of violent crime. In VRET, patients are exposed to simulated environments that recreate the traumatic events they experienced, allowing them to confront and reprocess their emotions. Through VR, therapists can gradually expose patients to these situations, offering them a controlled environment where they can experience the event at their own pace and develop coping strategies.

Example:

In **PTSD treatment for veterans**, VR is used to simulate combat situations, where patients can confront and **process their emotions** in real-time. The patient is guided by a therapist through the simulation, gradually reducing anxiety and fear associated with the trauma. Over time, this method can help patients reduce the severity of PTSD symptoms and improve their ability to cope with stressful situations.

2. **VR for Anxiety and Phobia Treatment:** VR is also being used in the treatment of **phobias** and **anxiety disorders**. By exposing patients to virtual representations of the things they fear—whether it's flying, spiders, or public speaking—VR therapy helps patients face their fears in a safe and controlled way. Through **graduated exposure**, patients can **desensitize themselves** to their triggers, ultimately reducing their anxiety and learning how to manage their responses in real-world situations.

   Example:

   A patient with a **fear of heights** might participate in a VR simulation where they are gradually exposed to higher altitudes—starting with virtual scenarios of standing on a low balcony, then advancing to a higher vantage point. Over time, the patient's anxiety decreases as they learn to manage their fear in controlled VR environments.

3. **VR for Learning and Empathy in Social Settings:** VR has also been used to teach **empathy** and

137

emotional intelligence in therapeutic and educational contexts. For example, **empathy training** programs use VR to simulate situations where individuals must interact with others in **emotionally charged** settings. Students or healthcare professionals can step into the shoes of a person with a specific mental health condition, such as **autism** or **dementia**, and experience the world from their perspective. This **emotional immersion** helps to build understanding and empathy, improving communication and care for those with these conditions.

Example:

In **virtual empathy training**, healthcare providers use VR to simulate interactions with patients suffering from dementia. The experience helps caregivers understand the emotional challenges faced by these patients, improving their ability to provide compassionate care.

This chapter has explored the psychological aspects of VR learning, highlighting the **cognitive benefits** of immersion, the **role of presence** and **emotional connection** in learning, and how VR is being used in therapeutic settings to promote healing and growth. Through its immersive nature, VR engages students on a deeper emotional and cognitive level, making learning not only more effective but also more meaningful. Real-world examples like **Virtual Reality Exposure Therapy** (VRET) and **empathy training** illustrate the powerful role VR can play in both education and psychological treatment, allowing individuals to confront fears, process trauma, and develop crucial life skills. As VR continues to advance, its psychological benefits will undoubtedly continue to revolutionize both education and therapy.

CHAPTER 16

VR AND GAMIFICATION IN EDUCATION

Turning Learning into an Adventure with Game Elements

The integration of **Virtual Reality (VR)** and **gamification** into education is transforming the way students engage with learning. By incorporating **game elements** into VR environments, educational content becomes more interactive, enjoyable, and engaging, turning traditional lessons into immersive adventures. This shift has the potential to make education feel less like a chore and more like a quest, enhancing the overall learning experience.

1. **Quest-Based Learning:** Gamification in VR allows educators to design **quest-based learning** experiences, where students embark on a series of challenges or missions to complete their education. These quests are typically structured with a narrative or storyline, which adds an element of **adventure** and **discovery**. As students progress through these

quests, they can unlock new levels, earn rewards, and uncover new content, much like they would in a traditional video game.

For example, in a **history lesson** on ancient civilizations, students might "travel" to ancient Egypt, where they must complete tasks such as solving puzzles related to the pyramids, learning about the culture, and interacting with virtual historical figures. Each completed task leads to the next part of the story, creating an engaging experience that feels like a journey.

2. **Game Mechanics in Education:** Gamification brings in essential **game mechanics**, such as **points**, **badges**, **leaderboards**, and **levels** that motivate students to keep progressing. These elements tap into intrinsic motivators such as **competition**, **achievement**, and **goal-setting**. As students complete educational tasks, they accumulate points or unlock badges, giving them a tangible sense of progress and accomplishment.

Leaderboards, where students can see how they rank against others, encourage a healthy form of

141

competition. While not all students are motivated by competition, this feature can drive **healthy peer comparison**, motivating students to improve their performance. The ability to unlock new levels or challenges further keeps students invested in their learning, as they feel a sense of anticipation and excitement for what's to come.

3. **Interactive Environments and Simulations:** VR's immersive nature adds another layer to gamification by allowing students to actively interact with the game environment. Rather than watching a lesson or reading a textbook, students can "physically" engage in the content, whether it's solving puzzles, completing a virtual treasure hunt, or performing experiments in a simulated lab. The use of **interactive tasks** ensures that students are not passive participants but active learners who must use critical thinking and problem-solving skills to succeed in the game.

4. **Narrative Storytelling:** One of the most engaging elements of gamification in VR is **narrative storytelling**, where the educational content is woven into an overarching story. This helps students form a deeper emotional connection to the material, making

it feel less like traditional learning and more like an adventure they want to embark upon. Stories within VR educational games can be customized to match students' interests, helping them remain engaged with the content and encouraging them to continue learning as they follow the narrative.

How Gamification Improves Motivation and Retention

Gamification is not just about adding fun elements to education—it's a powerful strategy for boosting **motivation** and improving **retention**. By incorporating game mechanics and **interactive elements** into the learning process, students are more likely to stay engaged, retain information, and feel a sense of accomplishment throughout their learning journey.

1. **Increased Motivation:** One of the primary benefits of gamification is its ability to keep students motivated. The **immediate rewards** (such as points, badges, and achievements) that come from completing tasks create a **positive feedback loop**. As students gain rewards, they feel more motivated to continue working towards the next goal, which keeps them engaged with the subject matter.

143

VR gamified education also allows for the creation of **fun challenges** that transform learning into a game. The idea of winning a game or leveling up is a powerful motivator that keeps students engaged, even in subjects that might otherwise feel tedious or difficult.

2. **Improved Engagement:** Gamified VR environments make learning more **interactive** and **hands-on**, encouraging students to actively participate in their education. This is much more engaging than passive forms of learning, such as reading from a textbook or listening to a lecture. Active participation, problem-solving, and interaction with the VR world increase cognitive engagement and **focus**, making it easier for students to absorb and retain new information.

3. **Higher Retention Rates:** Studies have shown that students retain information better when they are actively involved in the learning process, especially when they can see the immediate application of what they're learning. In gamified VR environments, the combination of **active learning**, **engaging content**, and **real-time feedback** helps students retain what

they've learned much more effectively than in traditional classroom settings.

Additionally, VR allows students to **revisit lessons** at their own pace, reinforcing their learning. For example, if a student struggles with a particular subject, they can replay certain tasks or challenges in the VR game, reinforcing the material until they fully grasp it. The ability to experience a lesson multiple times in an immersive, interactive way solidifies the information in the student's memory.

4. **Collaborative Learning Through Gamification:** Gamification doesn't just enhance individual learning—it can also encourage **collaborative learning**. In VR environments, students can work together to solve puzzles, complete challenges, and achieve objectives, fostering teamwork and communication. This collaborative aspect of VR games mirrors **real-world applications**, where students must collaborate to solve complex problems, much like they would in professional settings.

Group-based gamified tasks also promote **peer learning**, where students can teach and learn from one another as they navigate the game. This fosters a **supportive learning community** that encourages mutual growth and collaboration.

Real-World Example: VR Educational Games for Children

Gamification has proven particularly effective for **younger learners**, who often thrive in environments that allow them to explore, play, and learn in a fun, interactive way. **VR educational games** for children combine **learning objectives** with engaging game mechanics, creating a perfect blend of education and entertainment.

1. **ClassVR by Avantis: ClassVR** is a VR platform that uses gamification to engage children in subjects like science, history, and geography. The platform offers immersive VR experiences where children can visit **virtual field trips**, conduct experiments, or explore historical landmarks. The lessons are designed to be interactive and gamified, allowing students to earn points, badges, and rewards for completing challenges or answering questions correctly.

Example   in   Action:
Children learning about **the solar system** can embark on a VR mission where they travel to different planets, interact with celestial bodies, and complete puzzles that test their knowledge of the planets. As they progress through the game, they unlock new levels, gaining more in-depth knowledge about space while having fun exploring.

2. **Zoo VR: Zoo VR** is another educational game for children that uses **gamified learning** to teach them about animals, biology, and the environment. In this VR experience, children explore a virtual zoo, interact with various animals, and solve challenges related to animal habitats, diets, and behavior. The more tasks the children complete, the more animals they can unlock and learn about.

This gamified approach helps children develop a **curiosity** for biology and environmental science while also teaching them important facts about wildlife conservation. As children engage in these VR adventures, they gain knowledge in an interactive and fun way, reinforcing key concepts and ensuring better retention.

3. **Math in VR:** Several VR platforms are dedicated to making subjects like **math** more engaging and fun for children. For example, **VR Math World** uses VR to turn abstract mathematical concepts into interactive puzzles and games. Children can explore geometry, solve equations, and tackle math challenges by navigating through 3D environments, making math feel like an adventure rather than a difficult subject.

As students solve problems and complete math-based tasks, they earn rewards and unlock new levels, creating a sense of achievement and encouraging them to continue exploring and learning. This gamified approach helps children develop **math skills** in an enjoyable and immersive way.

This chapter has highlighted the integration of **gamification** and **VR** in education, showing how turning learning into an adventure with game elements can significantly enhance **motivation**, **engagement**, and **retention**. By using **game mechanics**, such as points, rewards, and challenges, VR helps make education more interactive, personalized, and enjoyable. Real-world examples, such as **ClassVR** and **Zoo VR**, demonstrate how gamification can transform traditional learning, especially for children, by providing them with immersive and interactive experiences that turn education into a fun and rewarding adventure. As VR and gamification continue to evolve, their potential to revolutionize education will only increase, making learning more engaging and effective for students of all ages.

CHAPTER 17

VR IN SPECIAL EDUCATION

The Potential of VR for Children with Learning Disabilities

Virtual Reality (VR) has opened new doors for students with **learning disabilities**, offering a powerful, immersive platform that adapts to their unique needs. In traditional classrooms, students with learning disabilities may struggle to engage with content through conventional methods. However, VR offers the potential to create **personalized learning experiences** that can significantly improve engagement, comprehension, and skill development.

1. **Engagement Through Immersive Environments:** Children with learning disabilities often struggle with traditional forms of instruction because they may have difficulty focusing, processing information, or staying engaged. VR offers a more **dynamic learning environment** that actively involves students by engaging multiple senses— sight, sound, and touch. These immersive environments hold the attention of students,

especially those who are prone to distractions. For example, students with **dyslexia** or **dysgraphia** can benefit from VR-based activities that incorporate **visual learning aids** and **interactive storytelling**, making learning more accessible and enjoyable.

2. **Hands-On Learning:** Many children with learning disabilities benefit from **hands-on learning**—an active, experiential approach that helps them grasp concepts more effectively than passive observation. In VR, children can interact with educational simulations in ways that would be impossible in a traditional classroom. For instance, children with **dyscalculia** can manipulate virtual objects to better understand mathematical concepts, while those with **dyslexia** can work on reading comprehension skills by interacting with visual and auditory cues in a virtual space.

3. **Safe Learning Environment:** For children with special needs, VR provides a **safe space** where they can learn, make mistakes, and experiment without fear of judgment or failure. The controlled nature of VR ensures that students can progress at their own pace and re-engage with lessons as many times as needed to build confidence. This is particularly

important for children who may face anxiety in conventional learning environments.

4. **Creating a Multisensory Experience:** VR enables the creation of a **multisensory experience** tailored to the specific needs of children with learning disabilities. For example, children with **auditory processing disorders** may benefit from VR environments where they can interact with sounds in a way that is clear and manageable. By incorporating multisensory elements, VR can help children with different needs focus on specific aspects of learning that they might otherwise struggle with in a traditional classroom setting.

Customized VR Programs for Autism, ADHD, and More

The power of VR in special education lies in its ability to be **customized** to meet the needs of individual students. For children with conditions like **Autism Spectrum Disorder (ASD), Attention Deficit Hyperactivity Disorder (ADHD),** or **dyslexia**, VR offers a way to design **tailored learning experiences** that address their specific challenges.

1. **Autism Spectrum Disorder (ASD):** VR has been particularly effective for students with **Autism**

Spectrum Disorder (ASD), as it provides a controlled and predictable environment in which they can practice social, communication, and behavioral skills. Students with autism often struggle with social interactions and understanding emotions in real-world settings. VR can simulate various social scenarios, allowing students to practice responding to social cues, interpreting facial expressions, and navigating conversations in a safe and low-pressure environment.

- o **Example:** A VR program might simulate a **grocery store environment** where a child with autism can practice how to ask for help, make purchases, or interact with other customers. The virtual environment can be designed to gradually introduce new social scenarios, helping the child build confidence and develop appropriate social behaviors.

2. **Attention Deficit Hyperactivity Disorder (ADHD):** Children with ADHD often face challenges related to **focus**, **impulsivity**, and **attention span**. VR's immersive and interactive nature can help **retain attention** and provide **structured activities** that keep students engaged.

153

VR allows students to complete tasks in a **gamified environment** that rewards focused attention and reinforces positive behavior.

- **Example:** In a VR-based math game, children with ADHD can solve problems and receive instant rewards or feedback. The immersive game world keeps the child's attention focused on the task, while the gamified elements, such as points or levels, encourage them to stay engaged and persist in solving problems.

3. **Dyslexia:** For children with **dyslexia**, VR can offer **visual aids** and **interactive reading exercises** that cater to their specific learning needs. VR can provide a more **dynamic, engaging approach** to reading by using visual representations and multisensory experiences, making it easier for students with dyslexia to understand word formation, spelling, and sentence structure.

- **Example:** A VR program designed for dyslexic students might feature a story where letters and words are represented visually in 3D, allowing the child to interact with the text by tracing letters or building words. By

154

associating sound, color, and movement with reading tasks, VR helps reinforce the connection between spoken and written language.

4. **Other Learning Disabilities:** VR can be customized to support other learning challenges, such as **dysgraphia** (difficulty with writing) and **dyspraxia** (difficulty with physical coordination). For example, VR can enable children with **dysgraphia** to practice handwriting by using virtual pens and interactive tracing tasks. Similarly, children with dyspraxia can engage in physical activities, such as virtual sports or exercises, to improve motor skills in a virtual environment that offers immediate feedback and encourages improvement.

Real-World Example: VR as an Educational Tool for Students with Autism

One of the most impactful applications of VR in special education is its use as a **therapeutic and educational tool for children with autism**. Through **VR simulations**, children with autism can practice critical social and cognitive skills in a safe, controlled space.

1. **The Virtual Reality Social Skills Training Program:** The **Virtual Reality Social Skills Training Program (VRSSP)** is a VR program developed to help children with autism improve their social interaction skills. The program immerses students in virtual scenarios where they can practice social interactions, such as initiating conversations, recognizing facial expressions, and responding appropriately to social cues.

   o **Example:** The program may simulate a scenario where a child with autism interacts with a virtual teacher or classmate, learning how to maintain eye contact, use appropriate greetings, and manage conversations. As the child becomes more comfortable with these scenarios, the virtual environment gradually increases in complexity, helping the child develop and reinforce positive social behaviors over time.

2. **VR Therapy for Anxiety and Stress Management:** Children with autism often experience **anxiety** and **stress** in unfamiliar or unpredictable situations. VR has been used as part of **cognitive behavioral therapy (CBT)** to help children with autism manage

156

anxiety and learn how to calm themselves in stressful environments. Virtual environments can be tailored to simulate **stress-inducing scenarios**, such as crowded spaces or loud noises, in a controlled and safe manner, allowing children to practice **coping strategies** without the risk of overwhelming them.

- o **Example:** A VR program might simulate a busy shopping mall, where the child can practice techniques like **deep breathing** or **self-talk** to calm down when they feel anxious. Over time, the program adjusts to the child's comfort level, reducing stress triggers and teaching them how to cope with real-life situations.

3. **Customized VR Educational Games for Autism:** Another real-world example is the use of **customized VR games** designed specifically for children with autism to develop essential skills. **Autism Glass**, for instance, is a VR-based game designed to teach children with autism how to recognize and respond to emotions. The game places students in virtual environments where they must identify facial expressions, tone of voice, and body language to understand how others are feeling. As they progress,

the game adjusts to the student's learning pace, offering **personalized feedback** and **rewards**.

- o **Example:** In this VR game, the student might encounter a virtual character who expresses sadness. The game prompts the student to identify the emotion and suggest appropriate responses, such as offering a kind word or asking if the character needs help. This type of interaction helps children with autism build empathy and emotional awareness.

This chapter has demonstrated how **Virtual Reality (VR) is** becoming a transformative tool in **special education**, particularly for children with **learning disabilities** such as **autism, ADHD,** and **dyslexia**. By creating **personalized learning environments** and offering **immersive experiences**, VR allows children to engage with educational content in a way that suits their unique needs. Real-world examples, such as VR-based social skills training programs and therapeutic tools for managing anxiety, highlight how VR is making education more inclusive and accessible. As VR technology continues to advance, its potential to support

students with special needs will expand, offering even more opportunities for personalized, effective learning.

CHAPTER 18

HOW VR IS CHANGING CORPORATE TRAINING

VR's Role in Corporate Education and Employee Development

Virtual Reality (VR) is reshaping the landscape of **corporate training** by offering innovative solutions that are immersive, cost-effective, and highly engaging. In traditional training environments, employees often sit through lectures, read manuals, or watch instructional videos—methods that are often passive and fail to capture the attention of participants. VR, on the other hand, transforms training into an **active, hands-on experience**, allowing employees to interact with their training materials and practice skills in realistic virtual environments.

1. **Immersive Learning Environments:** VR creates immersive environments that place employees into **real-world scenarios** where they can learn by doing. These virtual environments are designed to replicate

workplace situations, giving employees the opportunity to practice and learn in a controlled, risk-free setting. The immersive nature of VR increases engagement and makes training more memorable, helping employees retain information and skills more effectively than traditional methods.

2. **Cost-Effective Scaling:** Corporate training programs often require significant financial investments in resources such as physical materials, instructors, and travel expenses for on-site training. VR allows companies to create scalable training programs that can be accessed from any location, reducing costs associated with physical training sessions. Furthermore, employees can train at their own pace and revisit training modules as needed, ensuring continuous improvement without additional expenses.

3. **On-Demand Training and Flexibility:** VR training provides **on-demand access**, enabling employees to access training sessions at any time and from anywhere. This flexibility is particularly valuable for organizations with **global teams**, as it eliminates the need for scheduling conflicts and travel restrictions. Employees can complete training modules when it

suits their schedule, making it easier to integrate training into their day-to-day work without disrupting productivity.

4. **Personalized Learning Paths:** One of the key advantages of VR in corporate training is its ability to **personalize the learning experience**. Based on data from employees' performance within the VR training environment, companies can tailor the training program to focus on areas where employees need improvement. This level of personalization ensures that each employee receives the right amount of training for their skill level, whether they are beginners or experienced professionals.

5. **Remote and Global Training Solutions:** VR training provides companies with the ability to **train remote or geographically dispersed employees** without the need for physical meetings. Whether employees are working from home, in satellite offices, or traveling abroad, VR allows them to experience high-quality training regardless of their location, promoting consistency in training across different teams and regions.

Skill Building and Simulation for High-Stakes Professions

VR is especially valuable for **high-stakes professions** where employees need to acquire complex, specialized skills that require precision, confidence, and experience. In these fields, VR simulations provide **hands-on practice** in realistic, high-risk scenarios, allowing employees to develop their skills and **build muscle memory** before applying them in real-life situations.

1. **Training for Dangerous and High-Risk Jobs:** In high-risk industries such as **healthcare, construction, aviation,** and **military,** VR offers a safe, risk-free environment where employees can practice their skills without the danger of making mistakes. For example, in a **medical setting,** doctors and nurses can practice performing surgeries or managing medical emergencies in a virtual environment, allowing them to gain experience and confidence without the pressure of real-life consequences.

   Similarly, in **construction,** workers can practice handling hazardous materials, operating heavy machinery, and navigating construction sites—

without the potential for injury. VR allows these high-stakes professionals to gain valuable experience without putting themselves or others in danger.

2. **Simulations for Skill Mastery:** VR enables employees to simulate real-world tasks that require fine motor skills, decision-making, and quick reactions. For instance, in **aviation training**, pilots can practice landing and navigating aircraft in different weather conditions and emergency situations. Similarly, in **firefighting**, trainees can experience putting out a fire, rescuing people, and managing a crisis in a variety of environments, such as burning buildings, forests, or oil rigs.

   These immersive simulations provide an opportunity for employees to repeatedly practice and refine their skills in a **safe, controlled environment**, gradually building the competence needed to handle real-world challenges.

3. **Emotional and Situational Preparedness:** VR simulations are not just for technical skills—they also help employees develop **emotional preparedness** for high-stress situations. In industries

164

like **customer service**, **law enforcement**, and **emergency response**, employees must be able to handle intense situations, such as difficult customers or life-threatening emergencies. VR can simulate these high-pressure situations, giving employees a chance to practice their **emotional responses**, **communication skills**, and **decision-making** in real-time scenarios.

4. **Reinforcement of Safety Protocols:** In industries where safety is a primary concern, VR simulations reinforce the importance of **safety protocols** and **risk management**. Employees can experience potential hazards, such as electrical fires, toxic spills, or equipment malfunctions, and learn how to respond quickly and effectively in these high-risk situations. Through repeated exposure to safety scenarios in VR, employees internalize the steps they need to take, improving their response times and reducing the likelihood of accidents.

Real-World Example: Virtual Reality for Workplace Safety Training

Workplace safety training is one of the most important areas where VR has made a significant impact. By simulating real-life workplace hazards and emergencies, VR helps employees learn how to react appropriately in dangerous situations. This type of training is particularly valuable in industries like construction, manufacturing, and healthcare, where safety is critical.

1. **Walmart's VR Safety Training:** One of the most prominent examples of VR being used for workplace safety training comes from **Walmart**, which uses VR technology to train employees in **safety procedures**. Walmart partnered with **STRIVR**, a company that specializes in VR training, to create virtual simulations that teach employees how to handle various in-store situations, such as spills, fires, or other safety hazards.

   In these VR simulations, employees can navigate through **virtual stores**, encountering realistic safety challenges, like wet floors, hazardous material spills, or even customer accidents. As employees react to these situations, the VR system provides **immediate feedback** on their responses, helping them learn the proper safety protocols. This immersive, hands-on approach allows employees to gain real-world experience without actually being in a potentially dangerous situation.

2. **BP's VR Training for Oil Rig Workers:** Another example is **BP**, which uses VR to train **oil rig workers** on emergency procedures and safety protocols. Working on an oil rig can be dangerous, and VR training provides employees with a safe way to practice emergency evacuations, fire suppression, and other high-risk operations. In these simulations, employees must react to scenarios such as oil rig fires, gas leaks, or equipment failures, helping them gain experience in handling emergencies and ensuring that they are well-prepared for real-world situations.

The VR training helps employees practice **situational awareness**, decision-making under pressure, and teamwork, all of which are critical for ensuring the safety of everyone on the rig. By practicing these skills in a virtual environment, employees can make mistakes without real-world consequences and reinforce the right behaviors before facing actual emergencies.

3. **Health and Safety Training in Manufacturing:** In the **manufacturing industry**, companies like **Ford** have adopted VR to train workers on safety procedures, particularly for handling machinery, operating forklifts, and managing hazardous materials. In Ford's VR training program, employees can experience **virtual factory environments** where they must operate machinery and respond to potential hazards, such as equipment malfunctions, electrical fires, or chemical spills.

These VR simulations help employees become familiar with the machinery and the layout of the factory floor, so they know how to respond quickly in case of an emergency. Additionally, by using VR, employees are able to **retrain** and **revisit** safety protocols whenever necessary, reinforcing the importance of safety in the workplace.

This chapter has demonstrated how **Virtual Reality (VR) is transforming corporate training**, offering immersive, **real-world simulations** that improve employee **engagement**, **motivation**, and **performance**. Through

168

high-stakes skill-building, **safety simulations**, and **interactive scenarios**, VR prepares employees for complex tasks, enhances their abilities, and reinforces critical safety protocols. Real-world examples from companies like **Walmart**, **BP**, and **Ford** illustrate how VR is being used effectively to train employees in industries ranging from retail to oil and gas, ensuring that they are well-prepared for the challenges they may face on the job. As VR technology continues to evolve, its role in **corporate education and employee development** will only expand, offering new and more effective ways to train the workforce of the future.

CHAPTER 19

THE FUTURE OF VR IN EDUCATION

Emerging Trends and Innovations in VR Education

As **Virtual Reality (VR)** continues to evolve, its potential in education is expanding rapidly. New innovations are making VR learning experiences more immersive, accessible, and tailored to individual needs. These emerging trends promise to reshape the educational landscape, providing opportunities for deeper engagement, personalized learning, and interactive simulations across a variety of subjects.

1. **Integration of Artificial Intelligence (AI) with VR:** One of the most exciting trends in VR education is the integration of **Artificial Intelligence (AI)** with VR systems. AI can be used to create adaptive learning environments that respond in real-time to a student's actions, providing personalized feedback, adjusting difficulty levels, and tailoring the content

170

to each learner's unique needs. AI-driven **virtual tutors** and **avatars** can simulate real-world interactions, such as helping students solve problems or guiding them through complex tasks, ensuring a truly personalized learning experience.

2. **Multisensory VR Experiences:** As VR technology advances, there will be an increased focus on creating **multisensory learning environments** that go beyond just sight and sound. For example, **haptic feedback** (touch sensation) and **olfactory technology** (smell) are being developed to add more sensory elements to VR environments. These innovations allow students to physically feel virtual objects, experience the sensation of wind or temperature, or even smell virtual environments, enhancing the overall immersion and engagement in the learning process.

For example, a VR lesson on **underwater ecosystems** could involve not only seeing vibrant coral reefs but also feeling the motion of water and experiencing the temperature of the ocean, providing a richer and more realistic educational experience.

3. **Cross-Platform VR Learning:** As VR technology becomes more mainstream, it will increasingly integrate with other **learning technologies** such as **augmented reality (AR)** and **mixed reality (MR)**. This cross-platform integration will allow students to seamlessly transition between physical and virtual worlds. For example, students might engage in **AR-based lessons** on their mobile devices, then move to a VR headset for deeper immersion into the material. This integration of VR with other immersive technologies opens the door for **hybrid learning** models that combine the best of both physical and virtual education.

4. **Social and Collaborative Learning in VR:** The future of VR education will emphasize **collaborative learning** in virtual spaces. VR will allow students from all over the world to interact in shared, immersive environments, where they can work together on projects, attend classes, or engage in group activities. Virtual campuses, where students can meet in virtual classrooms, collaborate on assignments, and engage with instructors in real-time, will become more common. This fosters a

sense of **community** and encourages **peer-to-peer learning**, even in remote or online learning settings.

5. **Expanding Access to Education with VR:** One of the most transformative benefits of VR in education is its ability to make high-quality learning experiences accessible to a global audience. As the technology becomes more affordable and widespread, VR has the potential to revolutionize education for underserved populations. Students in remote areas, those with disabilities, and individuals who lack access to traditional educational resources will be able to engage in immersive learning experiences that were previously unavailable to them.

For instance, students in developing countries could experience virtual field trips to historical landmarks or receive specialized training in subjects such as healthcare or engineering, overcoming geographic and financial barriers.

Predictions for VR's Role in Education Over the Next Decade

Looking ahead, the role of VR in education is expected to grow exponentially, with more **schools, universities**, and

corporate training centers integrating VR into their teaching methods. The following predictions offer a glimpse into the **future of VR education** over the next decade:

1. **Ubiquitous Integration of VR in K-12 Schools:** As VR becomes more affordable and accessible, it is predicted that **K-12 schools** will increasingly adopt VR for classroom learning. Virtual field trips, interactive lessons, and immersive simulations will become commonplace, replacing traditional textbooks and static learning tools. VR will allow teachers to create **dynamic** and **engaging** lesson plans, where students can explore topics like history, science, and literature in a more interactive and hands-on way.

2. **Fully Immersive Virtual Classrooms:** In the next decade, we may see the rise of **fully immersive virtual classrooms**, where students and teachers interact in virtual spaces just like they would in a physical classroom. Students will wear VR headsets to attend live lectures, participate in group discussions, and collaborate with their peers, all from the comfort of their own homes or remote locations. These virtual classrooms will create a sense of **presence** and **community**, overcoming the

174

limitations of current video conferencing tools like Zoom or Microsoft Teams.

3. **Expanding VR in Higher Education and Research:** Universities and research institutions are expected to continue integrating VR into **higher education** and **research programs**. VR will enable students in fields like **medicine, engineering,** and **architecture** to conduct **virtual labs**, design and test prototypes, and simulate complex real-world scenarios. For example, medical students could perform **virtual surgeries**, engineering students could test new designs, and architecture students could walk through their designs in 3D before constructing them.

   Research in fields like **neuroscience, psychology,** and **human-computer interaction** will also benefit from VR by enabling experiments that study human behavior, learning processes, and brain functions in a controlled virtual environment.

4. **AI-Powered VR Learning Assistants:** The next decade will likely bring the development of **AI-powered VR learning assistants** that will guide students through their educational journeys. These

virtual assistants will use AI to monitor progress, identify areas where students may need help, and provide personalized instruction in real-time. These systems will continuously adapt to students' learning needs, offering targeted exercises, hints, and feedback based on individual performance.

5. **Immersive Learning Beyond the Classroom:** As VR technology evolves, it will extend beyond traditional educational settings. **Immersive learning experiences** will be available in the workplace, where employees can engage in **on-the-job training** through VR simulations. For example, a **pilot** could practice flying different aircraft in virtual environments, or a **manufacturing employee** could learn how to operate complex machinery without being physically present. This ability to practice real-world skills in a virtual environment will be valuable for industries like **healthcare**, **manufacturing**, **engineering**, and **customer service**.

6. **Global Virtual Campuses and Cultural Exchange:** In the future, we may see the establishment of **global virtual campuses** where students from around the world can engage in **cross-cultural exchanges**, attend lectures from professors

globally, and collaborate with peers from diverse backgrounds. These campuses will offer an inclusive learning environment that promotes **cultural awareness**, **global collaboration**, and **shared learning experiences** that transcend physical borders.

Real-World Example: The Future of Fully Immersive Education Systems

Fully immersive education systems powered by VR are already taking shape in some educational institutions and private organizations. These systems create virtual worlds where students can learn, collaborate, and engage in interactive, hands-on learning activities. Some examples of how these systems are shaping the future of education include:

1. **The Virtual Reality Education Accelerator (VREA):** The **VREA** is an organization that works with schools, colleges, and universities to integrate VR into their curricula. Their vision includes a future where schools will offer **virtual campuses** where students can engage with content in **fully immersive environments**. In this future, VR headsets will

177

replace traditional textbooks, allowing students to virtually walk through historical events, conduct virtual science experiments, or practice language skills by conversing with avatars in simulated environments.

The VREA is already testing **VR-based classrooms**, where students are transported to digital worlds to experience subjects such as history, geography, and science. These experiences engage students on a deeper level, increasing retention rates and making education more exciting and relevant.

2. **Virtual Learning Platforms for Higher Education: Stanford University, University of Illinois**, and other prestigious universities have already started incorporating VR into their teaching methods. For example, **Stanford's Virtual Reality Lab** is experimenting with immersive classrooms and virtual field trips to historical landmarks or medical research environments. Students in fields like medicine, engineering, and business are using VR to simulate real-world scenarios that they cannot easily replicate in traditional settings.

By creating **virtual spaces** where students can collaborate, explore, and experiment, these universities are pioneering the future of education by making it more interactive and hands-on, bridging the gap between theory and practice.

This chapter has explored the **future of VR in education**, focusing on **emerging trends**, **innovations**, and predictions for the next decade. As VR continues to evolve, it is expected to play a major role in transforming education by creating **immersive, interactive, and personalized learning experiences**. The integration of **AI**, the development of **fully immersive virtual classrooms**, and the expansion of **VR in higher education** and **corporate training** will shape the educational landscape, offering students new opportunities for learning and growth. Real-world examples of virtual campuses and immersive learning platforms demonstrate that the future of education is moving toward a **global, accessible**, and **immersive learning environment**.

CHAPTER 20

BARRIERS TO WIDESPREAD ADOPTION OF VR IN EDUCATION

Technological, Financial, and Cultural Challenges

As Virtual Reality (VR) emerges as a powerful tool for enhancing education, its adoption has been hindered by several key barriers. While the potential for VR in the classroom is vast, there are still significant **technological**, **financial**, and **cultural challenges** that schools and institutions must overcome before VR can become a mainstream educational tool.

1. **Technological Challenges:** The integration of VR into education requires sophisticated **hardware** and **software**, and not all schools or institutions are equipped with the resources to support such technology. While VR headsets and computers have become more affordable, they are still not universally accessible in all educational settings.

- o **Hardware Requirements:** For a fully immersive VR experience, schools need to invest in **high-performance computers**, **VR headsets**, and **motion controllers**. These systems require strong computing power to run complex simulations smoothly. Many schools, particularly those in underfunded or rural areas, may not have the infrastructure to support VR technology.

- o **Software Development and Integration:** Educational institutions must also adopt or develop **customized VR software** that is both effective and relevant to the curriculum. However, creating or purchasing VR content that aligns with diverse subjects or grade levels can be complex and costly. Moreover, institutions must ensure that VR software is compatible with their existing teaching platforms and infrastructure.

2. **Financial Challenges:** One of the primary barriers to the adoption of VR in education is its **high initial cost**. While VR technology has become more affordable over time, the upfront costs of purchasing hardware, developing or acquiring educational

content, and maintaining the systems can be prohibitively expensive for many schools, especially those with limited budgets.

- o **Initial Investment Costs:** Schools must invest not only in VR headsets and computers but also in supporting infrastructure like upgraded Wi-Fi networks, power sources, and sufficient storage for digital content. For example, a VR classroom setup might require dozens of headsets, motion controllers, and high-performance computers, each of which can cost thousands of dollars.

- o **Ongoing Maintenance and Updates:** Maintaining VR systems involves regular software updates, hardware repairs, and potentially replacing outdated equipment. This ongoing cost adds up over time, making it difficult for schools to sustain VR programs without significant investment from educational boards, governments, or private donors.

3. **Cultural Challenges:** The adoption of VR in education is also impeded by cultural and **pedagogical resistance**. Many educators, parents,

and policymakers may not fully understand the potential benefits of VR or may be hesitant to integrate new technologies into traditional teaching practices. In many cases, there is a **lack of awareness** about how VR can complement and enhance existing educational methods.

- o **Resistance to Change:** Some educators may be reluctant to embrace VR because they are accustomed to conventional teaching methods, such as lectures, textbooks, and in-person classroom activities. The shift to **digital learning environments** may seem intimidating or unnecessary, especially if teachers are not trained in the use of VR technologies.

- o **Fear of Technology Replacing Teachers:** Another cultural barrier is the fear that VR may **replace human educators** rather than complement them. While VR can be an effective tool for certain aspects of learning, it cannot replace the critical role that teachers play in fostering emotional support, social interaction, and personalized instruction. Overcoming this misconception is essential

183

for gaining broader support for VR in education.

How Schools and Institutions Can Overcome These Obstacles

Despite the challenges, there are several strategies that schools and institutions can use to **overcome barriers** and facilitate the successful adoption of VR in education. By addressing technological, financial, and cultural hurdles, educators can unlock the full potential of VR as an educational tool.

1. **Phased Implementation and Pilot Programs:** Schools can start by implementing **pilot VR programs** to test the technology and assess its effectiveness in the classroom. These smaller-scale implementations allow institutions to identify potential challenges, gather feedback from teachers and students, and make adjustments before committing to large-scale adoption. For example, a school might start by using VR in a single subject, such as science or history, to evaluate its impact on student engagement and learning outcomes.

2. **Partnerships with Tech Companies and Educational Organizations:** Schools can seek

partnerships with **VR technology companies**, **nonprofits**, and **government agencies** to access resources, funding, and expertise. Many tech companies offer educational discounts, donations, or grants for schools looking to integrate VR into their classrooms. Collaborations with universities or research institutions can also help schools stay updated on the latest developments in VR technology and best practices for its implementation.

- o **Example:** Companies like **Oculus** (Facebook), **HTC**, and **Google** have partnered with schools to provide VR headsets and training resources at discounted rates. By leveraging these partnerships, schools can reduce the upfront costs associated with VR adoption.

3. **Training and Professional Development for Educators:** Effective use of VR in education requires **teacher training** and **professional development**. Schools should invest in training programs that help educators understand how to integrate VR into their curriculum, how to create engaging VR content, and how to manage and monitor student progress in virtual environments.

185

Providing teachers with ongoing support and resources will increase their confidence in using VR technology and help them fully leverage its potential.

4. **Leveraging Open-Source and Affordable VR Content:** Many organizations are creating open-source or affordable **VR educational content** that schools can use without the need to develop expensive custom software. Schools can also take advantage of **existing VR platforms** and applications that are already tailored to specific subjects, such as **Google Expeditions** (virtual field trips) or **Labster** (virtual science labs). By utilizing these resources, schools can offer immersive educational experiences without incurring high content development costs.

5. **Government and Community Support:** Governments and local communities can play a crucial role in overcoming the financial barriers to VR adoption. Through grants, subsidies, or dedicated funding programs, government bodies can help schools purchase VR equipment and software, ensuring that all students have access to immersive learning opportunities. Additionally, schools can engage local communities and donors to raise funds

for VR initiatives, demonstrating how the technology will enhance educational outcomes and prepare students for the future.

6. **Creating a Culture of Technological Acceptance:** Overcoming cultural resistance involves fostering a **culture of technological acceptance** within schools and educational institutions. This can be achieved through **awareness campaigns**, **workshops**, and **demonstrations** that showcase the benefits of VR in education. Schools should emphasize that VR is a tool to complement, not replace, traditional teaching methods. Engaging teachers, parents, and students in the VR adoption process will help them feel more comfortable and confident with the technology.

Real-World Example: The Cost of VR Implementation in Education

One of the most significant barriers to the widespread adoption of VR in education is its **cost**. The initial investment required for hardware, software, and infrastructure can be daunting, especially for underfunded schools. However, there are several real-world examples of schools and institutions that have successfully implemented VR systems, despite these financial challenges.

1. **The University of Illinois at Urbana-Champaign:**
   The University of Illinois has been at the forefront of **VR adoption in higher education**, with a strong emphasis on using VR for teaching engineering, architecture, and medical students. The university initially faced significant **cost barriers** to VR implementation, particularly for hardware and software development. However, through a combination of **grants**, **industry partnerships**, and **donations** from technology companies, the university was able to establish a **VR laboratory** equipped with high-end VR headsets and computing systems.

   The VR lab allows students to engage in **interactive simulations** related to their coursework, such as conducting virtual lab experiments, designing architectural models, or simulating medical procedures. By partnering with tech companies like **HTC** and **Oculus**, the university was able to **reduce hardware costs** while also gaining access to specialized VR software tailored to their programs.

2. **Clinton Public Schools (CPS) in Arkansas:**
   Clinton Public Schools, a district in rural Arkansas,

faced challenges in integrating VR into its classrooms due to budget constraints. However, by partnering with **Google Expeditions**, CPS was able to implement a **VR program** that provided students with virtual field trips to museums, historical landmarks, and natural wonders without the need for costly travel. Google Expeditions offered the district **affordable VR headsets** and **free access** to its extensive library of educational content.

Despite initial concerns about costs, CPS found that the educational value of VR outweighed the financial investment. Students who participated in VR lessons showed **increased engagement**, **better understanding of complex concepts**, and a stronger interest in subjects like history and science.

This chapter has explored the **barriers to widespread adoption of VR in education**, including **technological, financial**, and **cultural challenges**. By addressing these obstacles with **strategic planning, partnerships**, and **training**, schools and institutions can successfully integrate VR into their curricula and create more **immersive,**

engaging, and **personalized learning environments**. Real-world examples, such as the **University of Illinois** and **Clinton Public Schools**, demonstrate how schools are overcoming cost and resource challenges to provide students with cutting-edge educational experiences. As VR technology continues to evolve and become more accessible, it will undoubtedly play an increasingly important role in shaping the future of education.

CHAPTER 21

VR IN THE GLOBAL EDUCATION LANDSCAPE

How Different Countries are Implementing VR in Education

As Virtual Reality (VR) becomes an increasingly vital tool in modern education, different countries across the globe are adopting it in unique and innovative ways. The integration of VR into education is not only revolutionizing how students engage with content but also providing opportunities for more inclusive, accessible, and interactive learning. Countries worldwide are embracing this technology to address various educational challenges, enhance learning outcomes, and better prepare students for the future.

1. **United States: Leading the Charge in EdTech Innovation** The United States is one of the leading countries in terms of VR adoption in education. From K-12 schools to universities, VR has found its place in classrooms across the country. VR is being

191

integrated into schools through both public and private initiatives, and many institutions are experimenting with immersive learning tools to enhance student engagement and understanding.

- o **Example: California State University** (CSU) has implemented VR in several disciplines, including **medicine** and **engineering**. Medical students use VR simulations to practice surgeries, while engineering students use VR to design and test prototypes. California is also home to several **K-12 districts** that use VR for virtual field trips, allowing students to explore historical sites or ecosystems from their classrooms.

2. **China: Investing Heavily in VR Education** China has become one of the fastest-growing adopters of VR technology in education. The Chinese government has made significant investments in educational technology, with a focus on VR and AI to modernize the country's education system. The integration of VR in Chinese classrooms aims to bridge gaps in **rural education**, provide better educational experiences for **disadvantaged**

students, and introduce innovative learning methodologies.

- o **Example:** In **Chinese primary and secondary schools**, VR is being used for immersive learning in subjects like **history**, **geography**, and **science**. Virtual field trips to the Great Wall of China or undersea explorations allow students in rural areas, who might not have access to these experiences otherwise, to engage with the curriculum in exciting ways.

3. **United Kingdom: Integrating VR into Higher Education** In the UK, **higher education institutions** have adopted VR for both teaching and research. Leading universities, such as **Oxford** and **University College London (UCL)**, use VR for research in fields like **neuroscience**, **architecture**, and **history**. VR enables students to conduct experiments or walk through historical sites from anywhere in the world.

- o **Example:** At **Oxford University**, VR is used in **medical training** to allow students to perform complex surgeries in virtual environments. Similarly, **UCL** has used VR to teach **architectural design** by allowing students to walk through and interact with virtual 3D models of buildings, helping them understand the spatial and functional elements of their designs.

4. **India: Overcoming Barriers to Education with VR** India has begun using VR to tackle some of its education system's most pressing challenges, such as lack of access to quality resources in rural areas, teacher shortages, and low engagement. VR is being used to **enhance educational opportunities** and provide access to content and experiences that students in remote or underdeveloped regions would not otherwise have access to.

   o **Example: India's VR education initiative**, spearheaded by companies like **Tata Trusts**, allows students in rural and underserved areas to experience **virtual field trips**, interactive science lessons, and **language learning programs**. VR is also used to improve vocational training programs in fields such as **healthcare**, **agriculture**, and **mechanical engineering**, offering students a hands-on, realistic learning environment.

5. **South Korea: A Hub for EdTech Innovation**

South Korea is known for its innovation in **technology** and **education**, and VR is a key component of its vision for the future of learning. South Korea's **Ministry of Education** has made substantial investments in **EdTech**, including VR, with the aim of creating immersive, engaging, and flexible educational experiences for students of all ages.

- **Example:** South Korea's **Seoul Metropolitan Office of Education** has implemented VR in **science education**, where students use virtual labs to conduct experiments that would otherwise be too costly or dangerous in a physical setting. South Korea is also using VR for **foreign language learning**, allowing students to interact with native speakers in realistic environments.

Global Examples of VR Integration in Schools and Universities

The global landscape of VR in education features a wide range of innovative use cases, with different countries adopting VR to enhance teaching, improve engagement, and offer immersive educational experiences. Several institutions around the world are making strides in this area, proving that VR is a **universal tool** for improving educational outcomes.

1. **Singapore: Leading the Charge in VR Learning**
   Singapore is known for its forward-thinking approach to **education** and has become a model for VR adoption in the Asia-Pacific region. The city-state has integrated VR into both primary and secondary schools, as well as in **higher education**.
   - **Example:** The **Singapore University of Technology and Design (SUTD)** uses VR technology to teach **architectural design** and **urban planning**. Students can create 3D models of buildings, cities, and neighborhoods and then "walk through" them in virtual space, allowing them to visualize their designs and assess their practicality before implementation.

2. **Australia: VR in Vocational and Tertiary Education** In Australia, VR is being adopted primarily in **vocational education and training (VET)** programs. These programs train students for careers in fields such as **construction, healthcare,**

and **hospitality**, where hands-on experience is crucial.

- o **Example: TAFE Queensland**, an Australian vocational education provider, is using VR to simulate complex technical tasks in industries like **plumbing**, **electricity**, and **nursing**. Students can practice skills in virtual environments, improving their confidence and competence before entering the workforce.

3. **Finland: Education as a Global Leader in VR Integration** Finland, known for its progressive and innovative education system, is incorporating VR in schools to teach a range of subjects, from **history** to **technology**. Finnish schools emphasize **student-centered learning**, and VR fits seamlessly into this approach by offering **personalized and immersive learning experiences**.

- o **Example: Helsinki's Virtual School** is a pioneering institution that integrates VR into **classroom lessons**. The school uses VR to create interactive **field trips**, **virtual museums**, and **science labs**, providing students with experiences that are difficult to replicate in the physical world. Finland's education system is also using VR to teach **social studies**, where students can engage with virtual cultural environments and historical settings.

4. **France: Innovative Use of VR in Language Learning** France is leveraging VR for **language learning**, providing students with an immersive and effective way to practice **foreign languages**. The use of VR in **language immersion** programs allows students to converse with native speakers and engage in cultural experiences that enhance their learning.

   o **Example:** At **Lyon University**, students of **French as a second language** (FSL) use VR environments to interact with virtual French-speaking characters. This allows them to practice pronunciation, conversational skills, and cultural context in realistic virtual settings, such as French cafés or marketplaces, making language learning more natural and engaging.

Real-World Example: How VR is Used in Developing Countries

In developing countries, where access to high-quality education is often limited by financial or logistical challenges, VR is making a significant impact by providing affordable, scalable, and high-quality learning experiences. Several countries are using VR to overcome barriers such as **lack of infrastructure, teacher shortages**, and **geographic isolation**.

1. **Kenya: VR for Education in Rural Areas** In **Kenya**, VR is being used to improve educational access in rural and underserved regions. With limited resources and infrastructure, many schools struggle to offer interactive and immersive educational opportunities. VR provides an innovative solution to this challenge by bringing the classroom to life without the need for expensive equipment or travel.

   o **Example:** The **Kenya Virtual Reality Education Program** uses VR to give students access to **virtual science experiments, field trips**, and **cultural experiences**. For example, students can visit **historical landmarks** or explore **the solar system**—experiences that would otherwise be impossible due to financial constraints. VR is helping bridge the education gap by providing engaging content to schools that would otherwise lack resources.

2. **Uganda: Using VR for Vocational Training** In **Uganda**, VR is being used to train students in vocational fields such as **agriculture, construction,** and **healthcare,** providing valuable **hands-on training** that would be difficult to achieve through traditional methods. With VR, students can simulate real-life scenarios, gaining practical experience and knowledge that would help them in their careers.

   o **Example:** The **Uganda Vocational Training Program** uses VR to train **farmers** in modern farming techniques, allowing them to practice tasks such as irrigation management, crop rotation, and pest control in virtual environments. This approach allows them to gain valuable skills without the need for expensive equipment or real-life farming experience.

3. **India: VR as a Tool for Inclusive Education** In **India**, VR is being used to create **inclusive education programs** for students with disabilities.

Many schools in India lack the resources to offer specialized education for children with learning disabilities or physical impairments, but VR is helping to level the playing field.

o **Example:** The **Disability and VR Education Program** in India uses VR to provide **interactive learning experiences** for children with special needs. Students with **visual impairments, hearing impairments,** or **mobility challenges** can engage with virtual simulations that are tailored to their needs, such as virtual classrooms, virtual tours, and interactive lessons, offering them opportunities for learning that they might not otherwise have access to.

This chapter has explored how **different countries** are implementing **VR in education**, from **primary schools** to **universities**, with a focus on **global examples** and **real-world applications**. Countries like the **United States, China, South Korea,** and **India** are leveraging VR to improve educational access, enhance learning experiences, and overcome logistical challenges. In **developing**

countries, VR is providing unique opportunities for **rural students**, **students with disabilities**, and those in **underserved regions** to experience high-quality education. As VR technology becomes more affordable and accessible, its role in the global education landscape will continue to grow, making education more engaging, interactive, and inclusive for students around the world.

CHAPTER 22

LEGAL AND ETHICAL CONSIDERATIONS OF VR IN EDUCATION

Privacy, Data Security, and Student Safety

As Virtual Reality (VR) becomes an integral part of the education system, significant legal and ethical considerations must be addressed to ensure that students' rights are protected, and their safety is prioritized. The immersive and interactive nature of VR poses unique challenges related to **privacy**, **data security**, and **student safety**, making it crucial for educational institutions, policymakers, and technology providers to set clear guidelines and safeguards.

1. **Privacy Concerns in VR Education:** One of the primary concerns with VR in education is the collection of personal data. Many VR platforms collect sensitive information about students, including **behavioral data**, **learning preferences**,

and even **biometric data** (such as eye tracking and facial expressions). The collection of such data raises concerns about student privacy, particularly regarding how this data is stored, used, and shared.

- ○ **Example:** VR headsets and software can track how long a student spends on specific tasks, how they interact with virtual objects, and how they react emotionally to different content. If not properly managed, this data could be misused or accessed by unauthorized third parties, potentially violating student privacy.

- ○ **Regulation Needed:** Educational institutions must ensure compliance with privacy laws, such as the **Family Educational Rights and Privacy Act (FERPA)** in the United States, which regulates the access and release of student information. Schools should also adhere to local privacy regulations, such as **General Data Protection Regulation (GDPR)** in the European Union, which governs the collection and processing of personal data.

2. **Data Security:** Given that VR platforms often store large amounts of sensitive data, maintaining **robust data security** is essential. Data breaches can lead to the exposure of personal information, causing harm to students and eroding trust in VR technology as an educational tool.

   o **Example:** Hackers gaining access to student data, including personal information or academic records, could lead to identity theft or exploitation. Educational institutions and VR providers must ensure that **data encryption, firewalls**, and **regular security audits** are in place to protect against unauthorized access.

3. **Student Safety in Virtual Environments:** While VR provides an immersive learning experience, it also introduces safety concerns related to **physical space** and **mental well-being**. For instance, students wearing VR headsets might experience disorientation, dizziness, or nausea due to **motion sickness**, a common issue known as **cybersickness**. In addition, students could accidentally injure themselves by moving around too quickly or

bumping into objects in their physical environment while immersed in virtual spaces.

- o **Physical Safety:** To address physical safety concerns, schools should ensure that students use VR in a **safe, open space**, free from obstacles. Supervisors should be present to monitor students' interactions in the virtual environment, particularly for younger children.

- o **Mental Well-being:** Educators must also be mindful of the emotional impact of immersive content. Intense VR experiences, such as those simulating traumatic events or complex emotional situations, may trigger distressing emotions in some students. Proper **content warnings** and **breaks between VR sessions** should be implemented to mitigate these risks.

Ethical Issues in Virtual Learning Environments

In addition to legal considerations, there are a range of **ethical issues** that educators, students, and VR developers must navigate when using VR in the classroom. These issues concern the fair and responsible use of VR technology, the potential for bias in educational content, and the impact of VR on students' well-being.

1. **Bias and Inclusivity in VR Content:** One significant ethical challenge in VR education is the potential for **bias** in the content and experiences offered to students. VR systems, like any other educational tool, can unintentionally perpetuate biases based on **race**, **gender**, **disability**, or **socio-economic status**. For example, a VR simulation that portrays historical events or cultural traditions may not accurately represent marginalized communities or could present content from a biased perspective.

   o **Example:** If a VR history simulation primarily reflects the perspectives of one cultural group, it could exclude or misrepresent the experiences of other communities. Developers must ensure that VR educational content is **inclusive**, **diverse**, and **culturally sensitive** to avoid reinforcing stereotypes or marginalizing underrepresented groups.

2. **Ethical Implications of Immersive Learning:** The immersive nature of VR poses ethical concerns regarding how deeply students become engaged in

virtual environments. The ability of VR to evoke strong emotional responses means that students may form **emotional connections** to virtual content, characters, or scenarios. This can raise questions about the **authenticity** of students' emotional experiences and whether they are being manipulated by the technology.

- o **Example: In VR-based therapy** or **empathy training**, students might feel deep emotional connections to virtual characters or scenarios, which could have positive or negative effects. While VR can help develop empathy, educators must ensure that emotional responses are managed responsibly and that students are not unduly influenced or manipulated by virtual experiences.

3. **Long-Term Impact on Social Skills and Human Interaction:** Another ethical concern is the potential for VR to **displace face-to-face interactions**. As VR becomes a more integral part of the educational landscape, there is concern that students may become overly reliant on virtual environments, potentially diminishing their ability to engage in **real-world social interactions**.

o **Example:** In a VR classroom, students may interact with virtual avatars or AI-driven tutors rather than human peers or instructors. While VR allows for social interactions in virtual environments, it is essential to maintain a balance between digital and **physical** socialization to ensure students develop necessary communication and interpersonal skills.

4. **Informed Consent for Virtual Learning:** Given the amount of personal data collected during VR interactions, informed consent is a key ethical issue in VR education. Students (and their parents, in the case of minors) should be fully informed about what data will be collected, how it will be used, and how long it will be stored. Consent should be clear, voluntary, and given before engaging in VR learning sessions.

o **Example:** Schools should provide parents and students with **privacy policies** and **terms of use** that explain the data collection processes, including **biometric data**, **learning analytics**, and **user interactions**. Consent forms should be easily understandable and ensure that individuals know their rights regarding data access and usage.

Real-World Example: The Role of Consent and Data in VR Education

In recent years, several real-world cases have highlighted the importance of **informed consent** and **data security** in VR education. These cases underscore the need for **clear policies** and **responsible data practices** to ensure that VR technology is used ethically in educational settings.

1. **Google Expeditions and Student Privacy: Google Expeditions**, a VR educational tool used in classrooms around the world, has faced scrutiny regarding student privacy and data security. Google Expeditions allows students to go on virtual field trips, but the company collects data related to student interactions with the VR content. In response to privacy concerns, Google worked with schools to implement **clear consent procedures** for data collection and ensure compliance with **FERPA** (Family Educational Rights and Privacy Act).

- o **Example:** In districts using Google Expeditions, schools send consent forms to parents outlining what data is being collected and how it will be used. By obtaining informed consent, schools ensure that they are in compliance with privacy laws and that students' personal information is protected.

2. **The Implementation of VR in Canadian Schools:** In Canada, several school districts have integrated VR into their classrooms. However, educators have been cautious about how VR platforms handle sensitive data, particularly regarding the collection of **biometric information**. For example, some VR platforms that track **eye movement** or **facial expressions** to measure student engagement or emotional responses have raised concerns about student privacy.

   - o **Example:** Before implementing VR programs, Canadian school districts established **data protection protocols** to ensure that any biometric data collected by VR systems was anonymized and used solely for educational purposes. Additionally, consent forms were provided to parents and guardians, ensuring transparency and maintaining trust between schools and families.

3. **Privacy Issues with VR Headsets in UK Schools:** In the UK, VR adoption in schools has raised concerns regarding the **long-term storage** and **security** of student data. For example, when students wear VR headsets, their personal preferences and learning habits are often tracked, raising questions about how this data is protected. To address these concerns, schools have been proactive in establishing **data-sharing agreements** with VR providers to ensure compliance with the **GDPR** and other privacy laws.

   o **Example:** UK schools implementing VR programs have partnered with developers to **limit data collection** to essential metrics and **ensure that all data is encrypted**. They have also made efforts to provide teachers with tools to monitor how student data is being used, ensuring that it remains secure and that students' rights are respected.

This chapter has examined the **legal and ethical considerations** associated with VR in education, including the importance of **privacy, data security**, and **student safety**. As VR becomes more integrated into educational systems, it is crucial for institutions to navigate these challenges responsibly, ensuring that students' rights are protected and that the technology is used ethically. Real-world examples like **Google Expeditions** and VR adoption in Canadian and UK schools demonstrate the importance of **informed consent, transparency**, and **data protection** in maintaining trust and safety in virtual learning environments. As the use of VR in education continues to grow, addressing these legal and ethical considerations will be key to its successful integration.

CHAPTER 23

CREATING YOUR OWN VR LEARNING CONTENT

Tools and Platforms for Developing VR Educational Content

The ability to create custom VR learning content has become increasingly accessible due to a variety of **tools** and **platforms** that simplify the process of developing immersive educational experiences. Whether you are an educator looking to enhance your curriculum with VR or a developer working to create interactive learning environments, there are numerous tools available to help you design, build, and deploy virtual reality educational content.

1. **Unity and Unreal Engine:** Unity and Unreal Engine are the two most widely used **game development engines** for creating VR content. Both offer **powerful features** for designing interactive environments, simulations, and educational games.

   o **Unity** is known for its user-friendly interface, flexibility, and large community of developers. It supports various VR platforms, including **Oculus Rift**, **HTC Vive**, and **PlayStation VR**, and offers a wide range of tutorials and assets to help educators get started. With Unity, educators can design everything from simple virtual field trips to complex simulations of scientific processes.

- ○ **Unreal Engine** is another robust option, known for its high-quality graphics and performance. While Unreal Engine is often used for **high-end gaming** development, it also provides powerful tools for creating visually stunning and immersive VR environments. Its **Blueprint visual scripting system** allows non-programmers to develop interactive content, making it an ideal choice for educators without coding experience.

2. **Google Tilt Brush and Oculus Medium:** For more creative and artistic VR content, tools like **Google Tilt Brush** and **Oculus Medium** enable users to create **3D models** and **interactive artwork** directly in virtual space. While these tools are primarily aimed at **artists** and **designers**, they offer powerful

potential for educators to create engaging visual content for their students.

- ○ **Google Tilt Brush** allows users to paint and create 3D objects and environments in VR, making it perfect for **art teachers** or **STEM educators** looking to create interactive models for their students. Teachers can create immersive scenes and experiences that students can explore and interact with, such as virtual museums or anatomical models.

- ○ **Oculus Medium** is another tool that allows users to sculpt and mold 3D creations in virtual space. It's particularly useful for **3D modeling**, allowing educators to create custom simulations or interactive learning tools in subjects like **history**, **engineering**, and **biology**.

3. **Cospaces Edu: Cospaces Edu** is a platform designed specifically for educators to create and share **interactive 3D content** for VR. It offers an intuitive drag-and-drop interface, making it easy for teachers and students to create virtual environments without any coding experience. With Cospaces, teachers can design custom lessons, such as **virtual**

216

tours, **simulations**, and **interactive storytelling projects**.

- o Teachers can create spaces for students to explore, such as virtual ecosystems or ancient civilizations, and integrate interactive elements like quizzes, puzzles, or games. The platform also supports VR headsets, allowing students to experience these environments fully immersively.

4. **VR Education Software Platforms:** Several platforms are tailored to the educational space, providing tools for educators to create custom VR learning content with minimal technical knowledge. These platforms often come with pre-built templates and lesson plans that make VR content creation easy.

- o **Engage VR** is one such platform that allows educators to create **customized virtual classrooms** and **immersive learning experiences**. Teachers can build **virtual campuses**, conduct live VR lectures, and create interactive learning modules that students can explore in real-time.

- o **ClassVR** is another platform aimed at simplifying VR content creation for schools.

217

It offers an intuitive interface that allows teachers to create immersive learning modules, use pre-made educational content, and manage VR devices remotely.

5. **Blender (For 3D Modeling and Animation):** **Blender** is a free, open-source software for creating 3D models, animations, and visual effects. It's widely used by both professionals and hobbyists to create high-quality content for VR. Educators can use Blender to create custom models, simulations, or animations for VR environments.

   o **Example:** A history teacher could use Blender to create 3D models of historical landmarks or artifacts, which could then be explored in a VR simulation. Similarly, science teachers could create detailed simulations of biological processes, such as the **circulatory system** or **cell division**, and allow students to interact with and manipulate these models in virtual space.

How Educators and Institutions Can Create Custom VR Learning Experiences

Creating custom VR learning experiences involves several key steps, from understanding the educational goals to selecting the right tools, content development, and deployment. Here's a breakdown of how educators and institutions can design and implement VR learning experiences:

1. **Define the Learning Objectives:** Before diving into VR content creation, it's essential to clearly define the **learning objectives**. Educators must determine the purpose of the VR experience—whether it's to improve **knowledge retention**, encourage **hands-on learning**, simulate real-world scenarios, or engage students in **active problem-solving**. The objectives will guide the content and the design of the VR experience.

   o **Example:** A biology teacher might design a VR experience where students explore the human body. The objective could be to help students understand **anatomical structures** and how they work together, with interactive

219

elements such as quizzes or challenges along the way.

2. **Choose the Right VR Tools and Platforms:** Depending on the educational objectives, educators should choose the tools and platforms that best suit their needs. For simple virtual field trips or basic interactive content, platforms like **Google Expeditions** or **Cospaces Edu** are ideal. For more complex simulations or interactive content, tools like **Unity** or **Unreal Engine** might be necessary.

3. **Design Engaging and Interactive Content:** Effective VR learning experiences are **interactive** and **engaging**. Educators should design content that encourages **active participation** rather than passive observation. This can include problem-solving tasks, virtual exploration, or role-playing scenarios. Content should be **learner-centered**, providing students with the freedom to explore and interact with the virtual environment at their own pace.

   o **Example:** In a history class, students could take on the role of an explorer navigating through ancient Egypt, solving puzzles and discovering artifacts along the way. The content should also be **interactive**, allowing students to engage with the virtual environment and make decisions that impact the outcome.

4. **Integrate VR into the Curriculum:** To maximize the effectiveness of VR, it should be seamlessly integrated into the **curriculum**. Educators can use VR as a supplement to traditional learning methods, aligning VR content with the topics and concepts being taught in class. This approach ensures that students can make meaningful connections between virtual experiences and classroom lessons.

   o **Example:** A chemistry teacher might use VR to demonstrate complex chemical reactions that would be difficult or dangerous to perform in a physical lab. Students could conduct virtual experiments and observe the results in real-time, enhancing their understanding of chemical principles.

5. **Test and Iterate:** After creating the VR content, it's important to test the experience with students to gather feedback and identify any issues. Educators should observe how students interact with the VR environment, collect feedback on usability and engagement, and make adjustments to improve the

experience. Continuous iteration is key to ensuring that VR content is effective and aligns with learning goals.

6. **Deployment and Access:** Once the VR content is developed and tested, it's time to deploy it to students. Educational institutions need to ensure they have the necessary infrastructure to support VR—this includes providing access to VR headsets, compatible devices, and ensuring a stable network connection. For large-scale deployment, institutions can look into **cloud-based VR platforms** that allow for **remote access** to VR content from any location.

Real-World Example: VR Content Creation in the Classroom

In many classrooms around the world, educators are already creating their own VR learning content to engage students in new ways. One notable example of this is **Stanford University**'s **VR Education Program**, which empowers students and instructors to design custom VR simulations and virtual environments for teaching purposes.

1. **Stanford University's VR Projects:** Stanford has implemented VR content creation in various

academic disciplines, allowing students to design and build simulations as part of their coursework. One such project is the **Stanford Virtual Reality Lab**, where students and faculty collaborate to develop immersive VR content for courses in **architecture, engineering**, and **medical education**. Through this program, students have created VR simulations for everything from **virtual anatomy dissections** to **architectural walkthroughs** of their design projects.

- o **Example:** In the **Stanford School of Medicine**, students use VR to conduct virtual surgeries and medical procedures. The content is custom-designed by faculty and students, using tools like **Unity** and **Unreal Engine**, to simulate realistic medical scenarios for training purposes.

2. **High School VR Content Creation:** In high schools, educators are also using platforms like **Cospaces Edu** and **ClassVR** to design engaging VR lessons. A **high school history teacher** might create a virtual field trip to ancient Rome, allowing students to explore Roman architecture, interact with virtual historical figures, and test their knowledge through

quizzes embedded in the experience. By using simple drag-and-drop tools, teachers can build this content without prior VR development experience.

This chapter has highlighted how educators can leverage **tools and platforms** to create **custom VR learning content** that engages students in **interactive, immersive educational experiences**. Whether through **game engines** like **Unity** and **Unreal Engine**, creative tools like **Google Tilt Brush**, or VR-focused platforms like **Cospaces Edu**, educators have the ability to craft unique learning environments that bring abstract concepts to life. By following a structured process that includes defining learning objectives, choosing the right tools, and testing content, educators can create VR experiences that enhance student engagement, understanding, and critical thinking. Real-world examples from **Stanford University** and **high school classrooms** illustrate how VR content creation is already transforming education, enabling students and educators alike to push the boundaries of traditional learning.

CHAPTER 24

THE IMPACT OF VR ON STUDENT ENGAGEMENT AND MOTIVATION

How VR Changes How Students Learn and Interact with Material

Virtual Reality (VR) is revolutionizing the way students engage with educational content by offering a dynamic, immersive learning environment that traditional teaching methods cannot replicate. By placing students in interactive virtual environments, VR enables a more hands-on, experiential approach to learning. This shift fundamentally changes how students interact with material, making learning more engaging and impactful.

1. **Immersive Learning Environments:** Traditional learning often involves passive interaction with text, images, or videos. In contrast, VR creates immersive environments where students can actively participate in the learning process. Instead of reading about the

225

solar system or watching a documentary, students can virtually visit different planets, explore asteroids, and understand the scale and motion of celestial bodies firsthand.

- **Example:** In a **biology class**, instead of reading about the circulatory system, students can enter a virtual simulation where they "travel" through the bloodstream, observing red blood cells carrying oxygen and experiencing the dynamics of heartbeats and blood circulation in real-time.

2. **Active Participation and Interaction:** VR promotes **active learning** by requiring students to interact with the virtual content, making decisions, solving problems, and navigating through scenarios. This level of interaction fosters **deeper engagement**, as students are no longer mere spectators but active participants in the learning process. For instance, in a **history lesson**, students could virtually explore ancient ruins, engage with historical figures, and solve challenges related to cultural artifacts, immersing themselves in the content rather than just reading about it.

- **Example:** In **language learning**, students can engage in **virtual conversations** with AI-driven avatars, practicing vocabulary, grammar, and pronunciation in realistic scenarios like a café or a marketplace. This kind of interaction makes learning more practical and context-driven.

3. **Visualization of Complex Concepts:** Some topics, especially in **STEM fields** (Science, Technology, Engineering, Mathematics), are abstract and difficult to grasp using traditional methods. VR allows for the **visualization** of complex concepts in 3D, providing students with an intuitive understanding of things like molecular structures, mathematical equations, or physical laws.

   - **Example:** In **physics**, students can explore **forces** and **motion** by manipulating virtual objects. They can test how different materials react to forces like gravity, friction, or pressure, giving them a hands-on understanding of principles that are often hard to visualize on paper.

VR's Impact on Focus and Motivation

One of the most significant impacts of VR on education is its ability to significantly **increase student motivation** and **sustain focus** throughout lessons. Traditional teaching methods, such as lectures and textbook readings, can lead to disengagement, especially in subjects that are perceived as dry or challenging. VR, however, creates an environment where students are motivated to engage, explore, and participate.

1. **Enhanced Focus Through Immersive Learning:** VR environments immerse students fully in the material, which helps them stay **focused** and **engaged**. The sensory experience of being inside a virtual world reduces the likelihood of distractions, keeping students concentrated on the lesson. In contrast, traditional classroom settings often have various distractions, such as classmates or outside noise, which can divert attention away from the material.

   o **Example:** In a **virtual science lab**, students can experiment with chemicals and conduct virtual experiments without leaving their seats. The immersive nature of the VR environment keeps them engaged in the task at hand, with fewer opportunities for off-task behavior.

2. **Gamification and Reward Systems:** Many VR educational platforms incorporate **gamification** elements, such as earning points, unlocking achievements, or progressing through levels. These game-like features tap into students' intrinsic motivations, encouraging them to actively participate and complete tasks. By embedding challenges, rewards, and goals, VR helps students stay motivated to continue learning and to reach their full potential.

   o **Example:** In **math education**, VR platforms often turn problem-solving into a game where students earn rewards for completing equations or solving puzzles. As students progress, they unlock more challenging levels, providing a sense of accomplishment and encouraging them to continue learning.

3. **Instant Feedback and Progress Tracking:** VR platforms provide **real-time feedback** on students' performance, allowing them to instantly see the results of their actions. This immediate feedback

reinforces learning, helping students recognize their strengths and areas for improvement. Moreover, many VR systems track students' progress and adapt the content based on their performance, ensuring that the material stays challenging and motivating.

- o **Example:** In a **language-learning VR program**, students might interact with virtual characters to practice conversation skills. If they make a mistake, the system provides corrective feedback, encouraging them to try again and reinforcing learning through repetition.

4. **Exploring New Interests and Expanding Horizons:** VR allows students to engage with topics and experiences that may have been out of their reach before. Whether it's visiting **ancient Rome**, exploring the **deep sea**, or conducting experiments on Mars, VR offers opportunities for **exploration** and **curiosity**. The ability to visit distant or unreachable places can spark an interest in subjects that students might not have previously considered, ultimately increasing motivation.

- o **Example:** Students studying **geography** or **environmental science** can take virtual field trips to places like the **Amazon Rainforest** or the **Arctic**, experiencing the ecosystems firsthand and gaining a deeper understanding of the subject matter.

Real-World Example: High-Engagement VR Lessons for Secondary Education

Several schools have already implemented VR technology to boost student engagement and motivation. One such example is **Brooklyn's International High School** in New York, which uses VR to immerse students in **interactive lessons** across subjects such as history, science, and literature.

1. **History and Social Studies:** Students in **history classes** at International High School use VR to experience significant historical events in **3D**, such as walking through ancient civilizations like **Mesopotamia** or interacting with virtual representations of historical figures. By stepping into historical settings and seeing firsthand what life was like in different eras, students develop a deeper connection to the material. This level of engagement

231

helps students better understand and retain information, compared to traditional textbook learning.

> o **Example:** For a lesson on the **American Revolution**, students may "attend" a reenactment of the Boston Tea Party, where they can observe and interact with the environment and the characters involved. This not only helps them remember historical facts but also sparks a deeper emotional connection to the events being studied.

2. **Science and Virtual Labs:** The school also uses VR to conduct **virtual science labs**, allowing students to perform experiments that would be difficult or impossible in a physical lab due to safety concerns or resource limitations. Students can simulate chemical reactions, explore human anatomy, and test environmental science theories in a fully interactive, risk-free virtual space.

> o **Example:** A **biology class** might use VR to conduct dissections of virtual animals, allowing students to examine organs and body structures up close without harming any creatures. These types of VR experiences

make science more tangible and exciting, motivating students to delve deeper into the subject.

3. **Literature and Storytelling:** In literature classes, students use VR to enter the worlds of the novels they are reading. For instance, when studying **Shakespeare's "A Midsummer Night's Dream"**, students can explore the enchanted forest where the play takes place, interact with the characters, and visually experience the magical elements of the play. This immersive experience enhances their understanding of the text and increases their interest in reading.

   o **Example:** Students studying **classic literature** like **"The Odyssey"** can walk alongside Odysseus as he faces the challenges of his journey, helping them visualize the narrative and gain a deeper understanding of the cultural context and themes.

4. **Increased Participation and Collaboration:** VR lessons also encourage **collaboration** among students. In a **virtual classroom**, students can work together on tasks, such as building a 3D model,

233

solving a problem, or exploring a new environment. This fosters teamwork, communication, and problem-solving skills, which are essential for success in both academic and professional settings.

- o **Example:** During a **group project**, students might collaborate on a **virtual chemistry experiment**, where they work together to mix chemicals, observe reactions, and record data. The ability to interact with the content as a team enhances cooperation and makes the learning experience more dynamic.

This chapter has explored how **Virtual Reality (VR) is** impacting **student engagement** and **motivation** in education. By offering immersive, hands-on learning experiences, VR changes the way students interact with educational material, making learning more dynamic and interactive. The ability to visualize complex concepts, experience historical events, and engage in real-world simulations leads to higher levels of focus, participation, and excitement in learning. Real-world examples, such as those from **Brooklyn's International High School**, show the **power** of VR to create **highly engaging lessons** that boost motivation and enhance the overall educational experience for students. As VR continues to evolve, its role in education will only grow, offering new opportunities to engage and motivate students in ways that traditional methods simply cannot achieve.

CHAPTER 25

THE ROLE OF VIRTUAL TEACHERS AND ASSISTANTS

Can VR Replace Traditional Teachers?

The concept of **virtual teachers** and **AI assistants** in education has raised an intriguing question: **Can VR replace traditional teachers?** While Virtual Reality (VR) technology has the potential to greatly enhance educational experiences, it is important to recognize that VR should not be viewed as a **replacement** for human educators but rather as a **complementary tool** that enhances the teaching process.

1. **The Human Touch:** Traditional teachers provide much more than just instructional content; they offer **emotional support**, **mentorship**, and the ability to adapt lessons to the needs of individual students. Human teachers can recognize the **emotional state** of a student, provide encouragement, and adjust teaching methods in real-time based on student

236

feedback and classroom dynamics. These qualities are difficult to replicate in a virtual environment.

- o **Example:** A teacher might notice a student struggling with a concept and offer extra help or change the teaching approach to better suit the student's learning style. This personalized support is vital in fostering a positive learning environment, which is something that current VR or AI systems cannot fully replicate.

2. **Facilitating Social Learning:** Education is not just about absorbing information; it also involves social and emotional development. **Peer interaction, group discussions**, and **collaborative problem-solving** are integral components of the learning process that VR, while immersive, cannot fully replace. Human teachers facilitate these interactions, helping students develop essential **soft skills** like communication, teamwork, and empathy.

- o **Example:** In a classroom setting, students may work together on a project, discuss ideas, and offer feedback to one another, fostering skills that extend beyond academic learning. VR can create simulations of these

237

scenarios, but the nuances of human interaction are difficult to simulate in a virtual space.

3. **Ethical and Emotional Considerations:** A virtual teacher or assistant may lack the **emotional intelligence** that human educators bring to the classroom. Educators often recognize when a student is going through personal difficulties, and their ability to provide appropriate support—whether academic or emotional—is crucial to a student's overall success.

   o **Example:** When a student is struggling with personal issues, such as family problems or mental health challenges, a human teacher can offer understanding, resources, or even a safe space to talk. This emotional connection helps students feel valued, and it is a dimension of education that a virtual teacher cannot provide at the same level.

In conclusion, while VR and AI can provide educational content and simulations, they are unlikely to fully replace traditional teachers in the foreseeable future. Instead, these technologies should be viewed as **valuable tools** that enhance and complement human teaching rather than as substitutes.

The Rise of Virtual Educators and AI Teaching Assistants

In recent years, there has been a significant rise in the development of **virtual educators** and **AI teaching assistants**. These technologies offer new ways to support and augment the traditional education system by providing personalized, scalable learning opportunities. AI-driven systems can assist in automating routine tasks, answering student queries, and guiding learners through complex subjects.

1. **AI Teaching Assistants:** AI assistants are increasingly being integrated into education systems to support both teachers and students. These **virtual assistants** can help by answering questions, providing feedback on assignments, and even offering **personalized learning paths** based on individual progress. AI systems are particularly useful for automating administrative tasks that would typically take up much of a teacher's time, such as

grading assignments and tracking student performance.

- o **Example: Socratic by Google** is an AI-powered app that helps students with their homework. By using the camera on their phones, students can scan a problem (such as a math equation or science question), and the AI assistant provides step-by-step solutions, explanations, and related learning resources.

2. **AI-Powered Virtual Tutors:** AI tutors are designed to offer individualized instruction, adapting to a student's learning style, pace, and needs. These **virtual tutors** can provide support 24/7, giving students the flexibility to learn at their own pace and on their own time. AI tutors are particularly valuable in **subjects** like **math, language learning**, and **coding**, where students may need constant practice and feedback.

- o **Example: Duolingo**, a popular language learning app, employs AI to adapt its lessons to the learner's skill level, providing personalized challenges and feedback. The app also uses gamification to keep learners motivated, making the process of learning a new language engaging and fun.

3. **VR Teachers in Virtual Classrooms:** VR technology is being increasingly utilized to create **virtual classrooms** where AI-powered instructors teach and interact with students in immersive 3D environments. These VR teachers can deliver lessons, facilitate discussions, and guide students through complex simulations. The immersive nature of VR allows students to feel as though they are physically present in a classroom or virtual field trip, enhancing engagement.

   o **Example: ClassVR**, a platform designed for schools, integrates VR content with curriculum subjects such as science, history, and art. Through VR headsets, students can experience subjects firsthand, from exploring ancient Egypt to conducting virtual science experiments. In this environment, a virtual teacher might guide students through lessons, provide feedback, and monitor their progress.

4. **The Role of Virtual Educators in Lifelong Learning:** Virtual educators are also playing an increasingly important role in **lifelong learning**. As

241

more adults seek to improve their skills or transition into new careers, AI-powered virtual assistants and tutors can provide tailored support, ensuring that learning is continuous and flexible.

- o **Example: LinkedIn Learning** uses AI to recommend courses based on an individual's career goals, past learning patterns, and industry trends. These AI-driven recommendations help learners find the most relevant resources to improve their professional skills, ensuring they stay competitive in an ever-changing job market.

Real-World Example: Virtual Teachers in Language Learning Apps

One of the most successful applications of **virtual teachers** and AI assistants can be seen in the field of **language learning**. Many language learning apps use **virtual tutors** to provide personalized instruction, feedback, and motivation. These platforms combine AI with **gamification** to create an engaging learning environment that keeps students motivated and immersed in the language-learning process.

1. **Duolingo: Duolingo**, one of the most popular language learning apps, uses **AI** to provide tailored lessons and real-time feedback to students. The app tracks each learner's progress, adjusting the difficulty level and offering personalized lessons based on their strengths and weaknesses. The app also uses **gamification** to keep students motivated, rewarding them with points, badges, and streaks for completing lessons.

   o **Example:** Duolingo's AI-powered chatbots act as virtual conversation partners, helping students practice speaking and writing in the target language. These bots engage students in real-time dialogues, mimicking real-world conversations, allowing learners to practice practical language skills in a low-pressure, supportive environment.

2. **Babbel:** Another well-known language learning platform, **Babbel**, also employs virtual assistants to help learners practice their language skills. Babbel uses AI to adjust lessons based on a learner's performance, ensuring that each student receives content that is **relevant** and **challenging**. The app also includes voice recognition technology to help

students with pronunciation, providing instant feedback on their speaking skills.

- ○ **Example:** Babbel's AI-driven system can assess the learner's ability to pronounce new words correctly and provide immediate corrective feedback. By helping students build confidence in speaking the language, Babbel's virtual assistant encourages consistent progress and helps learners feel more comfortable using the language in real-life situations.

3. **Busuu: Busuu**, another popular language learning app, incorporates **human-like virtual teachers** to create an engaging and realistic learning experience. The app's AI-powered tutors are designed to simulate real-world conversations, helping students practice their speaking and comprehension skills in an interactive, conversational format.

- ○ **Example:** Busuu uses **speech recognition technology** to assess pronunciation and fluency, providing learners with feedback on how well they are speaking. Additionally, Busuu offers interactive writing exercises, where virtual tutors give feedback on grammar and sentence structure, further supporting the learner's development.

This chapter has explored the **role of virtual teachers and assistants** in education, discussing how **VR** and **AI** technologies are enhancing the learning process. While VR may never replace traditional educators, it serves as a valuable tool for complementing and enhancing teaching methods. The rise of AI-powered **virtual educators, tutors**, and **teaching assistants** demonstrates how technology can support personalized learning, automate administrative tasks, and engage students in new and innovative ways. Real-world examples, such as **Duolingo, Babbel**, and **Busuu**, show the powerful impact of AI and VR in **language learning**, where virtual educators are providing customized support, real-time feedback, and consistent motivation. As technology continues to evolve, the role of virtual educators will continue to expand, offering new opportunities for engaging and accessible learning.

CHAPTER 26

CHALLENGES IN VR-BASED ASSESSMENT AND EVALUATION

How to Assess Learning in a VR Environment

Assessing learning in a **Virtual Reality (VR)** environment presents unique challenges compared to traditional classroom assessments. While VR offers immersive, interactive learning experiences, it also requires new approaches to evaluate student performance and understanding. Assessments in a VR environment need to be **dynamic**, **personalized**, and **real-time**, ensuring that students' interactions within the virtual space are accurately evaluated to gauge their learning outcomes.

1. **Real-Time Performance Tracking:** One of the primary ways to assess student learning in VR is through **real-time performance tracking**. In traditional education settings, assessment is often based on written tests or quizzes. In VR, however, assessments can be designed to track a student's

interactions, decision-making, and overall engagement with the virtual content. This type of assessment provides a deeper insight into how well students are understanding and applying the material.

- o **Example:** In a **virtual chemistry lab**, students can perform experiments by interacting with virtual lab equipment and chemicals. The system can track their actions, such as whether they follow the correct steps, make the right adjustments, and complete the experiment successfully. This **interactive performance** can be measured in real-time, providing immediate feedback.

2. **Behavioral Metrics and Engagement Analysis:** In VR environments, educators can assess students based on **behavioral metrics**, such as how long they spend on tasks, how they interact with virtual objects, or their ability to complete complex challenges. VR platforms can also track **engagement levels** by monitoring a student's attention span and their ability to stay focused on the task. These metrics offer a more holistic view of student performance beyond the typical right-or-wrong approach to assessment.

o **Example:** In a **history simulation** where students explore ancient ruins, the system could track which areas of the virtual world the student spends the most time in, what they interact with, and whether they solve the puzzles or answer questions correctly. This data can give insights into the student's **engagement** and understanding of the material.

3. **Simulations and Scenario-Based Assessments:** VR enables **scenario-based assessments** where students are placed in realistic situations that require them to apply knowledge and skills. These simulations provide authentic assessment experiences, where students must make decisions, solve problems, or perform tasks in a virtual setting.

o **Example:** In **medical education**, students might be placed in a virtual hospital environment where they have to diagnose and treat patients. Their ability to correctly assess symptoms, choose appropriate treatments, and respond to emergency situations can be tracked and evaluated. The scenario-based nature of the assessment

248

makes it possible to evaluate a student's **critical thinking, problem-solving,** and **technical skills** in real-world contexts.

4. **Continuous Formative Assessment:** Traditional education often uses summative assessments like midterms or final exams to evaluate student learning. In VR, assessment can be **continuous**, with data collected over time based on how students interact with the learning environment. This approach allows for more nuanced feedback and personalized instruction, helping students improve their performance gradually.

   o **Example:** In a **language learning VR environment**, a student might interact with virtual characters, practicing pronunciation, grammar, and conversation. Over time, the system tracks their progress, providing feedback after each session and identifying areas for improvement, such as word pronunciation or sentence structure.

Tools for Testing and Evaluating Student Progress in VR

To effectively assess student learning in VR environments, educators must utilize specialized tools and platforms designed for **VR-based testing and evaluation**. These tools allow instructors to monitor student progress, provide feedback, and track performance in a more interactive and personalized manner than traditional testing methods.

1. **VR Platforms with Built-In Assessment Features:** Many VR platforms used in education come with **built-in assessment** features that allow educators to create interactive tasks and measure student performance in real time. These platforms typically provide **data analytics** to track student progress and generate reports based on individual or group performance.

   - **Example: ClassVR** is a popular platform that provides educators with the ability to create immersive learning experiences, track student interactions, and assess their progress in real-time. Teachers can create customized **quizzes** or **challenges** within the VR environment, which can be used to evaluate students' understanding of the subject matter.

250

2. **Data Analytics and Reporting Tools:** VR-based assessment tools often include powerful **data analytics** capabilities. These tools allow educators to analyze various metrics such as **engagement**, **decision-making**, and **task completion**. By evaluating the collected data, teachers can gain insights into a student's learning habits, areas of difficulty, and overall progress.

   o **Example:** In a **math VR program**, data analytics can track how many times a student revisits certain problems, how long it takes them to complete tasks, and whether they make the correct choices. Educators can use this data to provide targeted feedback, identify areas that need improvement, and adjust the learning experience accordingly.

3. **AI-Powered Feedback Systems:** The integration of **AI-powered feedback systems** within VR platforms can automate the evaluation process and provide **instant feedback** to students. These systems use AI algorithms to analyze student interactions and provide tailored feedback based on their performance. This reduces the need for manual

251

grading and allows for a more dynamic, real-time approach to assessment.

- o **Example:** In a **VR medical simulation**, an AI-powered system could assess how a student performs diagnostic tasks and offers real-time feedback on their choices. If the student makes an incorrect diagnosis, the system could immediately provide a hint or explain why the chosen treatment was not appropriate, helping the student learn from their mistakes.

4. **Interactive and Adaptive Testing Tools:** Some VR environments include **adaptive testing** tools that adjust the difficulty of the content based on the student's progress. These tools ensure that assessments remain challenging yet achievable, helping students stay engaged and motivated while accurately measuring their skills.

- o **Example:** In **engineering education**, VR platforms can adapt the difficulty of simulations based on how well a student performs in previous tasks. If a student is performing well in basic simulations, the system may introduce more complex challenges, ensuring the student is always engaged with appropriate-level content.

Real-World Example: VR-Based Assessments in Medical Education

Medical education is one of the most advanced fields in terms of VR-based assessment and evaluation. The ability to simulate complex medical scenarios in a safe, controlled environment provides students with valuable opportunities to practice their skills without the risks associated with real-life clinical settings. VR-based assessments in this field allow for **hands-on experience**, **real-time feedback**, and **simulated decision-making**.

1. **VR Simulations for Clinical Training:** Medical schools and institutions around the world have integrated **VR-based assessments** into their curricula to train students in clinical skills, such as diagnosis, surgery, and patient interaction. VR simulations allow students to practice their skills in realistic, risk-free environments where they can make mistakes and learn from them.

- Example: **Osso VR**, a platform that offers **surgical training simulations**, allows medical students and professionals to practice surgeries using VR headsets and haptic feedback systems. Students are required to perform procedures like **knee arthroscopy** or **spinal surgery** within a simulated environment, and their actions are evaluated in real time. Feedback is provided immediately, helping students understand their strengths and weaknesses.

2. **Simulation of Patient Scenarios:** In medical education, VR assessments often involve **patient interaction scenarios**, where students must diagnose, treat, and manage virtual patients. These simulations are designed to test students' **decision-making, diagnostic abilities**, and **communication skills** in realistic settings.

   - Example: The **VIST™ (Virtual Interactive Simulation Technology)** platform is used to simulate patient scenarios where medical students can interact with virtual patients, diagnosing and providing treatment. The system tracks the student's choices, such as the medications they prescribe, the treatments they recommend, and how they communicate with patients. This allows for both **technical assessment** (e.g., correct diagnosis) and **emotional intelligence assessment** (e.g., communication and empathy).

3. **Remote VR Medical Assessments:** In the context of **remote education**, VR assessments allow students to participate in training and evaluations without being physically present in a hospital or classroom. These remote evaluations provide flexibility while maintaining high standards of assessment.

   o **Example: The Mayo Clinic** has developed a VR-based assessment tool that allows students to complete medical assessments from remote locations. The tool evaluates students on various tasks, such as **clinical reasoning**, **patient interaction**, and **hands-on procedures**, ensuring that medical students and professionals can continue their education and assessments remotely.

This chapter has explored the **challenges of VR-based assessment** and how to overcome them. Assessing learning in a VR environment requires innovative approaches that measure student interactions, decision-making, and engagement in real time. Tools like **real-time performance tracking**, **AI-powered feedback systems**, and **adaptive testing** are essential for evaluating student progress effectively. The use of **VR in medical education** provides a compelling example of how these technologies can be applied to **clinical training**, offering students opportunities for hands-on practice and immediate feedback in simulated environments. As VR technology continues to evolve, its role in assessment and evaluation will likely become more sophisticated, offering more precise, personalized, and engaging ways to measure student learning outcomes.

CHAPTER 27

CONCLUSION: THE ROAD AHEAD FOR VR IN EDUCATION

Summing Up the Impact of VR on Learning

As we've explored throughout this book, Virtual Reality (VR) has proven to be a transformative force in the world of education. From the early stages of immersive simulations to today's advanced VR platforms, the technology has dramatically reshaped the way students learn, interact with content, and engage in hands-on experiences.

VR in education allows for **interactive, experiential learning** that moves beyond the limitations of traditional textbooks, lectures, and classroom settings. It empowers students to actively participate in their education by enabling them to **explore new worlds**, **engage with complex concepts**, and **practice skills** in a risk-free virtual environment. This approach not only enhances **knowledge retention** but also improves **problem-solving** and **critical**

257

thinking skills by encouraging students to **apply what they learn** in realistic scenarios.

By immersing students in environments that are visually and functionally engaging, VR makes it possible to **visualize abstract concepts**, **simulate real-world scenarios**, and provide hands-on experiences that would otherwise be difficult to replicate in the classroom. Whether it's conducting a **virtual science experiment**, exploring **historical landmarks**, or practicing **medical procedures**, VR brings learning to life in ways that traditional education methods simply cannot.

Moreover, VR has democratized access to education, enabling students in remote or underserved areas to experience quality learning experiences, regardless of their geographic location or available resources. As the cost of VR technology continues to decrease and accessibility increases, the potential for VR to **level the playing field** and provide educational opportunities to a broader population grows.

Looking Towards the Future of Education in the Metaverse

Looking ahead, the future of education is likely to be shaped by the continued integration of VR into the broader **Metaverse**—a collective, virtual space where education, social interaction, and digital experiences converge. The Metaverse will not only extend the capabilities of VR but also introduce new ways for students to interact, collaborate, and learn in ways that are more fluid, dynamic, and expansive.

In the Metaverse, **virtual campuses** will become the norm, where students from around the world can interact in real-time, attend lectures, collaborate on projects, and engage with instructors, all within a fully immersive virtual environment. These virtual campuses will be just as vibrant and interactive as traditional schools but will provide the added flexibility and scalability that comes with VR technology.

Students in the Metaverse will be able to **create their own learning paths**, choosing the courses, resources, and experiences that align with their interests and goals. Teachers, equipped with **AI-powered teaching assistants** and **virtual tools**, will be able to offer personalized instruction that adapts to each student's learning style, progress, and needs. Students will be able to attend virtual field trips to **space**, **ancient civilizations**, or **remote ecosystems**, experiencing educational content in ways that were previously impossible.

Additionally, the Metaverse offers a unique opportunity to **bridge the gap** between various learning communities, creating opportunities for **global collaboration**. Students from different parts of the world will be able to work together on projects, share insights, and learn from one another's diverse perspectives. This connectivity will lead to an **inclusive and diverse learning environment** where education is not confined by physical boundaries or cultural differences.

As more educational institutions, companies, and governments invest in the development of the Metaverse, we are on the brink of a **paradigm shift** in how we think about and engage with education. The integration of VR within this interconnected, immersive world will drive innovation in teaching and learning, making education more personalized, accessible, and engaging for everyone.

Final Thoughts: How VR Could Shape Tomorrow's Classrooms

The next generation of classrooms will be drastically different from those of today. Traditional rows of desks and whiteboards will give way to **virtual environments** that are **adaptive**, **interactive**, and **immersive**. As VR technology continues to evolve, students will have access to an education that is **engaging**, **interactive**, and **relevant** to the world they live in.

Teachers will not only facilitate learning but will also act as **guides** who lead students through immersive educational experiences. Instead of relying solely on textbooks or lectures, educators will use VR simulations to bring complex concepts to life. Whether teaching about **ancient history**, **scientific principles**, or **engineering** challenges, teachers will use VR to create environments where students can **experience** the material firsthand.

The future classroom will also be increasingly **inclusive** and **accessible**, breaking down barriers related to **geography**, **physical ability**, and **socioeconomic status**. Students who would have otherwise been excluded from certain educational experiences due to financial constraints or geographical isolation will have the ability to access world-class content and learn alongside their peers from all over the world.

In these virtual classrooms, education will become more **student-centered**, with personalized learning paths and real-time feedback. Students will have more control over their learning experiences, allowing them to explore topics in depth, solve real-world problems, and develop skills that are highly relevant to the future job market.

Real-World Example: What the Next Generation of Students Will Experience

As we look towards the future, we can already see glimpses of what the next generation of students will experience in their educational journeys, thanks to early adopters of VR technology.

1. **Medical Education in VR:** One of the most impactful examples of VR in education can be seen in the field of **medical training**. Institutions like **Johns Hopkins University** and **Stanford University** have integrated VR into their curricula,

allowing medical students to perform virtual surgeries, interact with digital patients, and practice complex procedures in a safe, controlled environment. The next generation of medical students will likely have access to these technologies from the outset of their education, allowing them to gain **hands-on experience** in real-world medical situations long before they ever step into a hospital.

2. **Virtual Campuses and Global Classrooms:** Virtual reality will also revolutionize the concept of **higher education**. The next generation of university students will be able to attend **virtual campuses** and **global classrooms**, where they will interact with peers from around the world in real-time. Instead of being limited to the resources available on their own campus, students will have access to a **global network** of expertise and knowledge. They could study in **virtual labs**, attend **global guest lectures**, and collaborate on projects with teams located across continents—all within the immersive space of the Metaverse.

    o **Example: Arizona State University (ASU)** has already developed a virtual campus where students can attend classes, collaborate

263

with others, and engage in activities, regardless of their location. This platform allows students to attend classes virtually, attend events, and participate in simulations of real-world scenarios.

3. **The Rise of VR Learning in Secondary Schools:** For secondary education, VR offers a more engaging way to teach subjects like **history**, **science**, and **literature**. Students will have access to **interactive virtual tours** of historical landmarks, explore **distant planets** in science class, and step into the worlds of their favorite **novel characters**. This will not only enhance their understanding of complex concepts but will also foster a deeper **emotional connection** to the material, increasing both **motivation** and **engagement**.

   o **Example: The London School of Economics** (LSE) has already begun to explore the use of VR for teaching students from secondary education in underdeveloped regions. By using VR, students from remote or disadvantaged areas can experience the **same learning** opportunities as their counterparts in well-resourced schools.

264

This chapter has explored the immense potential of VR in education and its impact on the future of classrooms. The road ahead will see the evolution of **immersive learning** environments where students will be able to engage with their education in a **personalized**, **dynamic**, and **interactive** way. With VR, the barriers to access and engagement will be minimized, allowing education to become more **inclusive** and **global**. As we move into the Metaverse, the next generation of students will experience a vastly different kind of education—one that is immersive, collaborative, and deeply connected to the world around them. The future of learning is unfolding, and VR will undoubtedly play a central role in shaping tomorrow's classrooms.